DOCTOR · WHO

COMPANIONS AND ALLIES

STEVE TRIBE

BBC
BOOKS

10 9 8 7 6 5 4 3 2 1

Published in 2009 by BBC Books, an imprint of Ebury Publishing
A Random House Group Company

The Random House Group Limited Reg. No. 954009
Addresses for companies within the Random House Group can be found at www.randomhouse.co.uk

A CIP catalogue record for this book is available from the British Library.

ISBN 978 1 846 07749 4

The Random House Group Limited supports The Forest Stewardship Council (FSC), the leading international forest certification organisation. All our titles that are printed on Greenpeace approved FSC certified paper carry the FSC logo. Our paper procurement policy can be found at www.rbooks.co.uk/environment.

Commissioning Editor: Albert DePetrillo   Cover and interior design: Lee Binding
Project Editor: Kari Speers   Production Controllers: Antony Heller and Phil Spencer
Creative Consultant: Justin Richards

Printed and bound by Firmengruppe APPL, aprinta druck, Wemding, Germany.

BBC Books would like to thank the following for providing photographs and for permission to reproduce copyright material. While every effort has been made to trace and acknowledge all copyright holders, we would like to apologise should there have been any errors or omissions. All images copyright © BBC, except:
Page 7 (centre) Raymond P. Cusick
Page 42 (main image) The Braxiatek Collection
All computer-generated imagery courtesy of The Mill, including those on pages 63 (bottom left), 64 (bottom right), 66 (top right), 67 (top), 81 (inset), 87 (Adipose) and 95 (centre).

With additional thanks to:
Russell T Davies, Barnaby Edwards, David J. Howe, Glenn Ogden, Nicholas Payne, David Richardson, Edward Russell, Gary Russell, Jim Sangster, Tom Spilsbury and Peter Ware.

CONTENTS

COMPANIONS AND ALLIES

Donna Noble… Martha Jones… Rose Tyler… The Doctor has always sought out and befriended the most astonishing and amazing people, and helped them to fulfil their potential. From our very first encounter with him, travelling with his granddaughter, to his adventures on San Helios with Christina de Souza, the Doctor has had ordinary yet extraordinary people at his side. Wherever and whenever he goes, he has an impact on the people he meets, inspiring them to feats of heroism and showing them a better way to lead their lives.

The majority, of course, have kept their feet firmly rooted on the ground after meeting the Doctor – their lives transformed and often saved, they have remained on their home worlds and in their own times, a little safer and a little freer than they were before the Time Lord's arrival. Some have gone on to become leaders and peace-makers among their own peoples. And, just sometimes, the best of them have found themselves whisked away to a whole new life of adventure.

The Doctor has had many different travelling companions, who have joined him for all sorts of reasons. Some have, at first, been unwilling travellers, like Ian and Barbara or Tegan. Sometimes he has accepted responsibility for those left without protection or family, such as Victoria or Nyssa. Some, like Jo or Romana, have been thrust upon him; others, like Harry or Jamie, have been invited to join him. There have even been those who

have simply stumbled into the trip of a lifetime, like Dodo or Peri. All, though, have grabbed at that unique opportunity to visit other worlds, see strange skies and stranger creatures, and join the Doctor's constant quest for adventure and justice. They never give up, they don't just let things happen, they make a stand. They have the guts to do the right thing, when everyone else runs away. The Doctor only takes the best.

Among them have been real heroes, ready, for the Doctor's sake and for ours, to make any sacrifice – the heroes that most of us have only dreamed of becoming. Since the Time War, we have seen Rose, determined to stand by the Doctor's side, risk her life as she absorbed all the power of the Vortex and defeated the Daleks. The entire human race was saved from the Master and the Toclafane only thanks to Martha's year-long solitary trek across the planet. And Donna, the temp from Chiswick, for one shining moment was the universe's saviour. This book is a celebration of those ordinary, extraordinary people, and an introduction to those who have become the Doctor's friends, helping, assisting and sometimes rescuing him as he explores time and space.

'You act like such a lonely man,' Sarah Jane Smith told the Doctor. 'But look at you! You've got the biggest family on Earth!'

SUSAN FOREMAN

Played by Carole Ann Ford **First appearance** An Unearthly Child (1963) **Last regular appearance** The Dalek Invasion of Earth (1964) **Guest appearance** The Five Doctors (1983)

As the BBC Drama department prepared its new science fiction series, plans were drawn up for the four leads. Among these would be Biddy, 'a with-it girl of 15, eager for life'. By the time the first episode was transmitted, the part had been developed further – producer Verity Lambert and director Waris Hussein cast Carole Ann Ford as Susan, still 15, but now 'born in another world, another time'. Ford had already appeared in several TV serials as well as a film version of The Day of the Triffids.

When the Doctor fled Gallifrey in his stolen TARDIS, he was accompanied by his 15-year-old granddaughter, Susan. Together they explored Revolutionary

France, 19th-century England and Ancient Greece, met Pyrrho, Henry VIII and Beau Brummel, and saw metal seas and telepathic plants on planets like Venus, Esto and Quinnis. Settling in London for five months in 1963, the Doctor attempted to repair the TARDIS while Susan enrolled at the local school using the surname Foreman.

Susan was brilliant at some subjects, notably history, maths and science, but unfamiliar with Britain's pre-decimal currency, and there were other odd gaps in her knowledge. This and the erratic quality of her homework provoked the curiosity of two of her teachers,

Story **An Unearthly Child** ✪ Written by **Anthony Coburn** ✪ Featuring **the First Doctor, Ian, Barbara and Susan** ✪ Foe **cavemen** ✪ First broadcast **23 November–14 December 1963** ✪ 4 episodes

Story **The Daleks** ✪ Written by **Terry Nation** ✪ Featuring **the First Doctor, Ian, Barbara and Susan** ✪ Foe **the Daleks** ✪ First broadcast **21 December 1963–1 February 1964** ✪ 7 episodes

Story **The Edge of Destruction** ✪ Written by **David Whitaker** ✪ Featuring **the First Doctor, Ian, Barbara and Susan** ✪ First broadcast **8–15 February 1964** ✪ 2 episodes

Ian Chesterton and Barbara Wright, who investigated her home address – a junkyard containing a strangely humming police box…

Ian and Barbara discovered that their pupil was actually an alien from another time, with knowledge and skills far beyond their own understanding. Susan could read at phenomenal speed and could sometimes communicate telepathically. She was also growing up and was rapidly becoming more independent. Since they'd left their home world, Susan had been taking care of her grandfather as much as he'd been looking after her, and the Doctor eventually recognised that she needed a life of her own.

He left Susan in 22nd-century London, where she married David Campbell, a resistance fighter against the Daleks.

THE THALS

When Susan's teachers forced their way into the TARDIS, the Doctor hurriedly left Earth, taking his unwilling fellow travellers to the planet Skaro. This was the Dalek home world, its atmosphere still saturated with the radioactive fallout of a centuries-long war. With Ian, Barbara and the Doctor all affected by the fallout, Susan returned to the TARDIS for anti-radiation drugs. There she made contact with the Thals, Skaro's other main species and the Daleks' enemies in the neutronic war. The Thals had out-evolved the radiation's mutating effects and become physically strong and attractive. They had also become farmers and pacifists but, after the extermination of their leader, Temmosus, Ian persuaded them to attack the Dalek city. The Daleks were defeated, and the Doctor, Ian, Barbara and Susan's names passed into Thal legend.

BARBARA WRIGHT

Played by **Jacqueline Hill**
First appearance **An Unearthly Child (1963)** Last appearance **The Chase (1965)**

Few at the BBC really expected this new teatime science fiction series to last, and Jacqueline Hill initially accepted just six weeks' work as the third regular, Lola. The character was renamed Barbara, a schoolteacher who found herself travelling through time, and Hill ultimately stayed for almost two years, alongside William Russell. In 1980, Hill returned to Doctor Who, though not as Barabara – in Meglos, she played Lexa, leader of the Deons on the planet Tigella.

A history teacher at London's Coal Hill School, Barbara's interest was piqued by her strange pupil Susan. Hoping to confront the girl's grandfather and tell him to take some interest in her, she instead stumbled into a two-year trip through time and space.

Barbara proved less sceptical than Ian when the Doctor explained that he and Susan were time travellers from another world. She always remained hopeful that the Doctor would return them to 20th-century London, but was practical enough to try to make the best of their situation. She revelled in the chance to experience history first-hand, from Kublai Khan's Cathay to Revolutionary Paris, but was also

Story **Marco Polo** ☻ Written by **John Lucarotti** ☻ Featuring **the First Doctor, Ian, Barbara and Susan** ☻ Foe **Tegana** ☻ First broadcast **22 February–4 April 1964** ☻ **7 episodes**

Story **The Keys of Marinus** ☻ Written by **Terry Nation** ☻ Featuring **the First Doctor, Ian, Barbara and Susan** ☻ Foe **the Voord** ☻ First broadcast **11 April–16 May 1964** ☻ **6 episodes**

Story **The Aztecs** ☻ Written by **John Lucarotti** ☻ Featuring **the First Doctor, Ian, Barbara and Susan** ☻ Foe **Tlotoxl** ☻ First broadcast **23 May–13 June 1964** ☻ **4 episodes**

THE AZTECS

Mistaken for a reincarnated Aztec god in a temple in 15th-century Mexico, Barbara attempted to persuade the high priests to end the practice of human sacrifice. Autloc, High Priest of Knowledge, was open-minded and proved receptive, although this was partly because he trusted that she was revealing the true will of his gods. In the face of concerted attempts by the High Priest of Sacrifice, Tlotoxl, to discredit the 'false god', Autloc remained loyal and frequently interceded on behalf of Barbara's friends. Ultimately, his faith almost broken, Autloc abandoned his office to help get Susan safely back to the TARDIS, before becoming a hermit in the wilderness beyond the city.

The Doctor also secured help among the Aztecs, though his efforts to charm the lady Cameca were more successful than he had expected – she accepted his apparent marriage proposal and was heartbroken when he left in the TARDIS.

Story **The Sensorites** ⊕ Written by **Peter R. Newman** ⊕ Featuring **the First Doctor, Ian, Barbara and Susan** ⊕ Foe **deranged spacemen** ⊕ First broadcast **20 June–1 August 1964** ⊕ **6 episodes**

Story **The Reign of Terror** ⊕ Written by **Dennis Spooner** ⊕ Featuring **the First Doctor, Ian, Barbara and Susan** ⊕ Foe **French revolutionaries** ⊕ First broadcast **8 August–12 September 1965** ⊕ **6 episodes**

Story **Planet of Giants** ⊕ Written by **Louis Marks** ⊕ Featuring **the First Doctor, Ian, Barbara and Susan** ⊕ Foe **Forrester** ⊕ First broadcast **31 October–14 November 1964** ⊕ **3 episodes**

aware of the dangers of the past – she knew how the Romans treated their slaves and understood the hazards of the 12th-century Crusades. She hoped time travel might give them a chance to put right history's mistakes, but the Doctor warned her that she could not rewrite a single line of history. This argument was one of several Barbara had with the Doctor, who initially viewed his uninvited guests with suspicion. When the TARDIS malfunctioned, the Doctor wrongly accused Ian and Barbara of sabotaging his ship, which Barbara deeply resented. But as the Doctor began to appreciate the qualities of his new travelling companions, his attitude towards them started to soften.

IAN CHESTERTON

Played by **William Russell**
First appearance **An Unearthly Child (1963)** Last appearance **The Chase (1965)**

The BBC wanted a strong and courageous young male lead to contrast with the older figure of the Doctor. 'Cliff' would be 'physically perfect' and 'even brainy'. By 1963, William Russell was already a well-known actor, whose many roles had included the leads in Nicholas Nickleby and The Adventures of Sir Lancelot, making him ideal for the renamed part of Ian. Russell and Hill left Doctor Who almost two years later, having starred in 77 episodes.

Story **The Dalek Invasion of Earth** ☺ Written by **Terry Nation** ☺ Featuring **the First Doctor, Ian, Barbara and Susan** ☺ Foe **the Daleks** ☺ First broadcast **21 November–26 December 1964** ☺ **6 episodes**

Story **The Rescue** ☺ Written by **David Whitaker** ☺ Featuring **the First Doctor, Ian, Barbara and Vicki** ☺ Foe **Koquilion** ☺ First broadcast **2–9 January 1965** ☺ **2 episodes**

Story **The Romans** ☺ Written by **Dennis Spooner** ☺ Featuring **the First Doctor, Ian, Barbara and Vicki** ☺ Foe **Nero** ☺ First broadcast **16 January–6 February 1965** ☺ **4 episodes**

Faced with the TARDIS interior and Susan's insistence that it was a time machine, Ian Chesterton's first response was disbelief. Naturally sceptical and inquiring, the science teacher needed proof, not the Doctor's condescending half-explanations. Given that proof – as the TARDIS took them to Stone Age Earth – Ian quickly admitted the reality of their situation. He was keen to understand how the TARDIS worked, though he accepted that the ship's systems were beyond him. He could be as stubborn as the Doctor, but Ian was always practical and generally took the lead as the four travellers tried to free themselves from cavemen or Daleks, once even leading a revolt

THE MENOPTRA

The peaceful, civilised inhabitants of the planet Vortis in the Isop galaxy, the Menoptra were a race of large insects resembling giant butterflies. When the TARDIS was drawn to Vortis, the Doctor, Ian, Barbara and Vicki found that the Menoptra had lost their world 200 years earlier to an invading Animus, which had enslaved the ant-like Zarbi and was slowly engulfing the planet with its web-city, the Carsenome. Most of the Menoptra had fled to a nearby moon. While Ian and Menoptra Vrestin fought to free the subterranean Optera, Barbara was rescued from the Zarbi by Menoptra Hrostar. The Animus was eventually destroyed in a combined assault by the time travellers and a small group of Menoptra.

among galley slaves in Ancient Rome. Ian felt responsible for Barbara and Susan's safety, and was willing to fight to defend them, or to defy the Doctor if his actions would endanger them. Ian enjoyed his adventures with the Doctor, seeing Napoleon's rise to power, being knighted by Richard the Lionheart and outwitting the Voord on Marinus. But his greatest wish was always to return home. He and the Doctor

had their final disagreement when they found a time ship belonging to a defeated squad of Daleks, and Ian and Barbara realised they could use it to reach 20th century Earth.

Story **The Web Planet** ☻ Written by **Bill Strutton** ☻ Featuring **the First Doctor, Ian, Barbara and Vicki** ☻ Foe **the Animus, the Zarbi** ☻ First broadcast **13 February–20 March 1965** ☻ **6 episodes**

Story **The Crusade** ☻ Written by **David Whitaker** ☻ Featuring **the First Doctor, Ian, Barbara and Vicki** ☻ Foe **El Akir** ☻ First broadcast **27 March–17 April 1965** ☻ **4 episodes**

Story **The Space Museum** ☻ Written by **Glyn Jones** ☻ Featuring **the First Doctor, Ian, Barbara and Vicki** ☻ Foe **the Moroks** ☻ First broadcast **24 April– 15 May 1965** ☻ **4 episodes**

VICKI

Played by **Maureen O'Brien**
First appearance **The Rescue (1965)** Last appearance **The Myth Makers (1965)**

When Carole Ann Ford left Doctor Who after its first year, she was replaced by 21-year-old Maureen O'Brien, a founding member of Liverpool's Everyman Theatre. This was her first television role, and it came during the year of 'Dalekmania', when the series was enjoying some of its highest audience ratings.

Story **The Chase** ☻ Written by **Terry Nation** ☻ Featuring **the First Doctor, Ian, Barbara, Vicki and Steven** ☻ Foe **the Daleks** ☻ First broadcast **22 May–26 June 1965** ☻ **6 episodes**

Story **The Time Meddler** ☻ Written by **Dennis Spooner** ☻ Featuring **the First Doctor, Vicki and Steven** ☻ Foe **the Meddling Monk** ☻ First broadcast **3–24 July 1965** ☻ **4 episodes**

Story **Galaxy 4** ☻ Written by **William Emms** ☻ Featuring **the First Doctor, Vicki and Steven** ☻ Foe **the Drahvins** ☻ First broadcast **11 September–2 October 1965** ☻ **4 episodes**

A teenaged orphan from the late 25th century, Vicki was marooned on the planet Dido after a spaceship crash, one of just two survivors. Missing Susan, the Doctor promptly decided to offer Vicki a place on the TARDIS. The girl brought out a softer side in him, and he was a kindlier grandfather figure with her than perhaps he had been with Susan. Vicki relished meeting such famous figures from history as Nero and King Richard and enthusiastically joined in rebellions against tyrannical aliens like the Moroks. After a 25th-century education – lasting an hour a week and covering several subjects, including medicine, physics and chemistry – she was amused by Ian and Barbara's 20th-century outlook. But when she met and fell in love with Troilus during the Trojan Wars, she chose to leave the TARDIS and stay with him.

STEVEN TAYLOR

Played by **Peter Purves**
First appearance **The Chase (1965)** Last appearance **The Savages (1966)**

Having auditioned to play a Menoptra in The Web Planet, Peter Purves made his first appearance in Doctor Who in the third episode of The Chase as Morton Dill, a bemused tourist who encountered a Dalek at the top of the Empire State Building. With both William Russell and Jacqueline Hill leaving the series three episodes later, a new companion was required, and the production team quickly decided to offer Purves a regular role.

Steven Taylor was a spaceship pilot whose craft crashed on the planet Mechanus, where he was imprisoned by the Mechonoids, spherical robots left on the planet to make it suitable for human habitation. Steven was finally freed from his two-year captivity when the Daleks pursued the TARDIS to Mechanus. As the Daleks and Mechonoids fought, Steven found his way to the TARDIS. Steven was headstrong and independent, frequently clashing with the Doctor – he almost left the ship when the Doctor refused to alter history by saving a young girl from a massacre in 16th-century Paris – but he was also loyal, brave and decisive. When the TARDIS took them to a world where Elders were exploiting a race of Savages, Steven stayed there as the planet's new, unifying leader.

KATARINA

The handmaiden to Princess Cassandra in ancient Troy, Katarina briefly accompanied the Doctor after helping get the injured Steven back to the TARDIS. She had no understanding of the technological wonders she was seeing, and thought of the Doctor as a god who was taking her on a divine journey in his temple. She sacrificed herself in an attempt to save the Doctor from being forced to face the Daleks.

SPACE SECURITY SERVICE

In AD 4000, space agent Marc Cory died before he could warn Earth of a Dalek plot to gather a number of alien races into a force to attack the solar system. When the Doctor discovered that the Daleks had recruited the Guardian of the Solar System, Mavic Chen, members of the SSS were ordered to apprehend him. He and Steven managed to convince first Bret Vyon and then his sister Sara Kingdom to support them, but both agents died in the subsequent fight.

Story **Mission to the Unknown** ⊛ Written by **Terry Nation** ⊛ Foe **the Daleks** ⊛ First broadcast **9 October 1965** ⊛ **1 episode**

Story **The Myth Makers** ⊛ Written by **Donald Cotton** ⊛ Featuring **the First Doctor, Vicki, Steven and Katarina** ⊛ Foe **Greeks, Trojans** ⊛ First broadcast **16 October–6 November 1965** ⊛ **4 episodes**

Story **The Daleks' Master Plan** ⊛ Written by **Terry Nation, Dennis Spooner** ⊛ Featuring **the First Doctor, Steven and Katarina** ⊛ Foe **the Daleks, Mavic Chen** ⊛ First broadcast **13 November 1965–29 January 1966** ⊛ **12 episodes**

DODO CHAPLET

Played by **Jackie Lane**
First appearance **The Massacre (1966)** Last appearance **The War Machines (1966)**

Jackie Lane was offered the role of Susan when Doctor Who first entered production, but decided against accepting a year-long contract. By 1966, she had changed her mind and accepted a renewed offer of a regular part in the show.

Having stumbled into the TARDIS thinking it was a real police box, Dorothea Chaplet was totally unfazed when she stepped out into a jungle area aboard a huge space ark carrying humans and animals away from a doomed future Earth – Dodo assumed it was Whipsnade Zoo in England. She was excited but undaunted by each new landing, infuriating the Doctor and Steven by running off to explore before they were sure it was safe. Her speech, full of teenage slang, also irritated the Doctor, though she reminded him of Susan and he soon grew very fond of her. But Dodo was deeply affected when she was hypnotised by the supercomputer WOTAN and forced to work against the Doctor, and she decided to remain on Earth.

Story **The Massacre** ⊕ Written by **John Lucarotti** ⊕ Featuring **the First Doctor, Steven and Dodo** ⊕ Foe **French Catholics** ⊕ First broadcast **5–26 February 1966** ⊕ **4 episodes**

Story **The Ark** ⊕ Written by **Paul Erickson & Lesley Scott** ⊕ Featuring **the First Doctor, Steven and Dodo** ⊕ Foe **the Monoids** ⊕ First broadcast **5–26 March 1966** ⊕ **4 episodes**

Story **The Celestial Toymaker** ⊕ Written by **Brian Hayles** ⊕ Featuring **the First Doctor, Steven and Dodo** ⊕ Foe **the Toymaker** ⊕ First broadcast **2–23 April 1966** ⊕ **4 episodes**

POLLY WRIGHT

Played by **Anneke Wills**
First appearance **The War Machines (1966)** Last appearance **The Faceless Ones (1967)**

An actor from the age of 9, Anneke Wills was already well known from many television series and films, including The Railway Children and The Avengers, by the time she accepted the part of Polly. She and Michael Craze joined at the same time, and they jokingly marked Patrick Troughton's first day as the Doctor by wearing T-shirts proclaiming 'Come back Bill Hartnell, all is forgiven!'

When Polly met the Doctor, she was working as a secretary for the inventor of WOTAN. Though she was briefly hypnotised by the supercomputer, her loyalty to her friends overcame her conditioning. Polly was attractive, friendly and bubbly but, while some people thought she was just a dumb blonde, she was quite capable of using her looks to disarm and charm her way out of trouble, managing to tease and manipulate the English officer Algernon ffinch into helping her in the Scottish Highlands. Polly was frequently terrified by the Daleks, Macra, Chameleons and other monstrous creatures she encountered but, happy as she was to go and make the coffee, she was also perceptive enough to deduce a weakness in the Cybermen attacking the Moonbase – inspired by her nail varnish remover, she invented 'Cocktail Polly', a mixture of solvents that dissolved the plastic in their chest units.

Story **The Gunfighters** ☻ Written by **Donald Cotton** ☻ Featuring **the First Doctor, Steven and Dodo** ☻ Foe **Johnny Ringo, the Clantons** ☻ First broadcast **30 April–21 May 1966** ☻ **4 episodes**

Story **The Savages** ☻ Written by **Ian Stuart Black** ☻ Featuring **the First Doctor, Steven and Dodo** ☻ Foe **the Elders** ☻ First broadcast **28 May–18 June 1966** ☻ **4 episodes**

Story **The War Machines** ☻ Written by **Ian Stuart Black** ☻ Featuring **the First Doctor, Dodo, Ben and Polly** ☻ Foe **WOTAN** ☻ First broadcast **25 June–16 July 1966** ☻ **4 episodes**

BEN JACKSON

Played by **Michael Craze**
First appearance **The War Machines** (1966) Last appearance **The Faceless Ones** (1967)

Like Anneke Wills, Michael Craze already had several years' experience by the time he joined Doctor Who, having been acting professionally from the age of 12. In a break with the series' then fairly conservative approach, Craze was chosen to play a lower-class cockney sailor, inspired by Michael Caine's Alfie.

Able Seaman Ben Jackson only got involved with the Doctor because Polly took pity on him when she saw him sitting on his own in a nightclub. A strong friendship quickly developed, with Ben often making fun of Polly's accent and background, calling her 'Duchess', and Polly teasing Ben for his simple loyalty and obedience to the Navy and then to the Doctor. That was sorely tested when the Doctor regenerated, and Ben remained suspicious of the new Doctor long after Polly had accepted him. His automatic deference to authority was turned against him when the Macra conditioned him to work for them, though Ben's instinctive faith in his companions ultimately broke through. But Ben had been missing his naval posting when Polly met him, and he seized the chance to leave the TARDIS when they landed in England on the same day they had left.

Story **The Smugglers** ⊛ Written by **Brian Hayles** ⊛ Featuring **the First Doctor, Ben and Polly** ⊛ Foe **smugglers** ⊛ First broadcast **10 September–1 October 1966** ⊛ **4 episodes**

Story **The Tenth Planet** ⊛ Written by **Kit Pedler & Gerry Davis** ⊛ Featuring **the First Doctor, Ben and Polly** ⊛ Foe **the Cybermen** ⊛ First broadcast **8–29 October 1966** ⊛ **4 episodes**

JAMIE MACRIMMON

Played by **Frazer Hines** First appearance **The Highlanders (1966)** Last regular appearance **The War Games (1969)** Guest appearances **The Five Doctors (1903)** and **The Two Doctors (1905)**

When Frazer Hines was cast as James Robert Macrimmon in Patrick Troughton's second story, the production team were uncertain whether the character would work as a series regular, but Hines's performance during location filming convinced them to keep him on. As a result, Jamie played only a limited role in the next few adventures, with Hines often being given lines originally written for the other regulars. Hines stayed on for the whole of the Second Doctor's era, making Jamie one of Doctor Who's longest-running companions. Hines and Troughton became firm friends, renowned for playing practical jokes on their female co-stars, and Hines returned to the show twice for guest appearances in the 1980s.

The Doctor, Ben and Polly met Jamie in Scotland in April 1746, shortly after the Battle of Culloden. Jamie, a piper, was uneducated and uncomplicated but brave, resourceful and unwaveringly loyal to his clan chief. Having helped defeat a band of English slave traders, Jamie accepted the Doctor's invitation to join him on

Story **The Power of the Daleks** ☺ Written by **David Whitaker** ☺ Featuring **the Second Doctor, Ben and Polly** ☺ Foe **the Daleks** ☺ First broadcast **5 November–10 December 1966** ☺ **6 episodes**

Story **The Highlanders** ☺ Written by **Elwyn Jones & Gerry Davis** ☺ Featuring **the Second Doctor, Ben, Polly and Jamie** ☺ Foe **slave traders** ☺ First broadcast **17 December 1966–7 January 1967** ☺ **4 episodes**

Story **The Underwater Menace** ☺ Written by **Geoffrey Orme** ☺ Featuring **the Second Doctor, Ben, Polly and Jamie** ☺ Foe **Professor Zaroff** ☺ First broadcast **14 January–4 February 1967** ☺ **4 episodes**

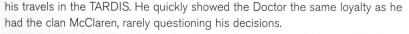

his travels in the TARDIS. He quickly showed the Doctor the same loyalty as he had the clan McClaren, rarely questioning his decisions.

Jamie never forgot his Highland roots, usually carrying a dirk, a small knife, and always wearing his kilt, even on the snowy peaks of the Himalayas. Though clearly happy to wander the universe with the Doctor, he never lost his love of his country – when the TARDIS became trapped in a Land of Fiction, he was lured out of the ship by false images of the Highlands. Even after several years of time travel, his first response to the sight of an English Redcoat was to attack, a weakness exploited by the Master of the Land of Fiction. With the battle cry 'Creag an tuire', Jamie was never averse to leaping into action to defend his friends. He was especially protective of Victoria Waterfield, who he rescued from the Daleks. Jamie's relationship with Zoe Heriot was a little more sparky and competitive, as Jamie struggled to cope with concepts that she and the Doctor understood with ease. Zoe delighted in catching him out as he pretended to know what she was talking about, though perhaps she underestimated how much he sometimes worried

Story **The Moonbase** ☻ Written by **Kit Pedler** ☻ Featuring **the Second Doctor, Ben, Polly and Jamie** ☻ Foe **the Cybermen** ☻ First broadcast **11 February–4 March 1967** ☻ **4 episodes**

Story **The Macra Terror** ☻ Written by **Ian Stuart Black** ☻ Featuring **the Second Doctor, Ben, Polly and Jamie** ☻ Foe **the Macra** ☻ First broadcast **11 March–1 April 1967** ☻ **4 episodes**

Story **The Faceless Ones** ☻ Written by **David Ellis & Malcolm Hulke** ☻ Featuring **the Second Doctor, Ben, Polly and Jamie** ☻ Foe **the Chameleons** ☻ First broadcast **8 April–13 May 1967** ☻ **6 episodes**

about the Doctor thinking less of him. Jamie frequently tried to relate his new experiences to things he knew from home. When he first saw a Cyberman, he took it to be the Phantom Piper, a mythical figure that appeared to dying members of his clan. Arriving at Heathrow in 1966, he was astonished to see metal 'flying beasties' taking off from the airport runways.

Jamie was actually very quick to benefit from his experiences. This was noted by the Dominators, who examined his brain and found signs of recent rapid learning. He learned to read while with the Doctor, and came up with schemes to capture a robot Yeti and to intercept a bomb on its way to the core of the planet Dulkis.

When the Time Lords caught up with the Doctor, however, they returned his companions to their homes. Jamie was taken to the Highlands, at a point just before he had first entered the TARDIS, removing his memories of all but his first adventure with the Doctor.

Story **The Evil of the Daleks** ۞ Written by **David Whitaker** ۞ Featuring **the Second Doctor, Jamie and Victoria** ۞ Foe **the Daleks** ۞ First broadcast **20 May–1 July 1967** ۞ **7 episodes**

Story **The Tomb of the Cybermen** ۞ Written by **Kit Pedler & Gerry Davis** ۞ Featuring **the Second Doctor, Jamie and Victoria** ۞ Foe **the Cybermen** ۞ First broadcast **2–23 September 1967** ۞ **4 episodes**

Story **The Abominable Snowmen** ۞ Written by **Mervyn Haisman & Henry Lincoln** ۞ Featuring **the Second Doctor, Jamie and Victoria** ۞ Foe **the Yeti, the Great Intelligence** ۞ First broadcast **30 September–4 November 1967** ۞ **6 episodes**

PROFESSOR TRAVERS

An anthropologist and explorer, Edward Travers led an expedition to the Himalayas in 1935 in search of the legendary Abominable Snowmen. What he found were robot Yeti controlled by the Great Intelligence, which were attacking the monastery of Det-Sen as the first stage in a planned conquest of Earth. Travers initially betrayed the Doctor to the monks, but soon realised his mistake and helped end the invasion.

Almost 40 years later, Travers was recruited as the army's scientific adviser when robot Yeti took over the London Underground and spread a deadly fungus through the city.

VICTORIA WATERFIELD

Played by **Deborah Watling**
First appearance **The Evil of the Daleks (1967)** Last appearance **Fury from the Deep (1968)**

Deborah Watling was the daughter of Jack Watling, who played Professor Travers in the two Yeti stories. As a child actress, she had already appeared in several television serials and plays in the 1950s, including The Invisible Man, and had recently played Alice in The Life of Lewis Carroll when she won the role of Victoria.

Though she accepted the Doctor's invitation to board the TARDIS after the Daleks killed her father, Victoria was an unwilling traveller. Facing Cybermen, Yeti and Ice Warriors in quick succession, she spent much of her time scared and screaming – something the Doctor turned to his advantage when he amplified her screams to destroy a weed creature.

She also constantly missed her father and her 19th-century home life. When she had the chance to settle in England in the late 20th century and become part of a new family, she quickly took it.

Story **The Ice Warriors** ☻ Written by **Brian Hayles** ☻ Featuring **the Second Doctor, Jamie and Victoria** ☻ Foe **the Ice Warriors** ☻ First broadcast **11 November–16 December 1967** ☻ **6 episodes**

Story **The Enemy of the World** ☻ Written by **David Whitaker** ☻ Featuring **the Second Doctor, Jamie and Victoria** ☻ Foe **Salamander** ☻ First broadcast **23 December 1967–27 January 1968** ☻ **6 episodes**

Story **The Web of Fear** ☻ Written by **Mervyn Haisman & Henry Lincoln** ☻ Featuring **the Second Doctor, Jamie, Victoria and Lethbridge-Stewart** ☻ Foe **the Yeti, the Great Intelligence** ☻ First broadcast **3 February–9 March 1968** ☻ **6 episodes**

ZOE HERIOT

Played by **Wendy Padbury** First appearance **The Wheel in Space (1968)** Last regular appearance **The War Games (1969)** Guest appearance **The Five Doctors (1983)**

A former regular on TV soap Crossroads, Wendy Padbury joined the TARDIS for Patrick Troughton's final season. Five years later, she played another companion – Jenny – on stage in the theatre production Doctor Who and the Daleks in Seven Keys to Doomsday, and returned as Zoe for The Five Doctors in 1983. A first-class astrophysicist and astrometricist aboard a 21st-century space station, the Wheel, Zoe had a reputation among her colleagues as

being all brain and no heart. She had a photographic memory and a complete faith in logic – which, the Doctor told her, 'merely enables one to be wrong with authority'. Realising that there might be more to life, she stowed away aboard the TARDIS. She, Jamie and the Doctor went on to battle Cybermen, Dominators, Quarks, Krotons, Ice Warriors and space pirates before the Time Lords returned her to the Wheel.

Story **Fury from the Deep** ☻ Written by **Victor Pemberton** ☻ Featuring **the Second Doctor, Jamie and Victoria** ☻ Foe **weed creature** ☻ First broadcast **16 March–20 April 1968** ☻ **6 episodes**

Story **The Wheel in Space** ☻ Written by **Kit Pedler** ☻ Featuring **the Second Doctor, Jamie and Zoe** ☻ Foe **the Cybermen** ☻ First broadcast **27 April–1 June 1968** ☻ **6 episodes**

Story **The Dominators** ☻ Written by **Norman Ashby** ☻ Featuring **the Second Doctor, Jamie and Zoe** ☻ Foe **the Dominators, the Quarks** ☻ First broadcast **10 August–7 September 1968** ☻ **5 episodes**

BRIGADIER LETHBRIDGE-STEWART

Played by **Nicholas Courtney** First appearances **The Web of Fear** and **The Invasion (1968)** First regular appearance **Spearhead from Space (1970)** Last regular appearance **Terror of the Zygons (1975)** Guest appearances **Mawdryn Undead** and **The Five Doctors (1983)**, **Battlefield (1989)**

Having appeared as Bret Vyon in the First Doctor story The Daleks' Master Plan, Nicholas Courtney was cast by director Douglas Camfield as Colonel Lethbridge-Stewart for The Web of Fear. Later the same year, Doctor Who established its own military intelligence taskforce and Courtney was brought back to reprise his role, with Lethbridge-Stewart promoted to Brigadier. Courtney was a regular in the early years of Jon Pertwee's time as the Doctor and went on to appear in adventures with the Fourth, Fifth and Seventh Doctors. In 2008, Courtney returned once again as Sir Alistair Gordon Lethbridge-Stewart, this time in The Sarah Jane Adventures, helping to defeat the Bane and a lone Sontaran.

Alistair Gordon Lethbridge-Stewart first encountered the Doctor in the London Underground during the Yeti invasion. At first suspicious of the Doctor, Colonel Lethbridge-Stewart had to concede that the Great Intelligence's attack could not have been repelled without him.

Four years later, having been promoted to Brigadier and appointed head of the British branch of UNIT (see box), Lethbridge-Stewart again relied on the Doctor's help, this time to defeat an invasion by the Cybermen. It was the start of a very long friendship.

UNIT

This special intelligence taskforce was formed in the aftermath of the Yeti invasion of the London Underground, its mission to investigate the odd and the unexplained and to defend Earth from alien threats. It drew its personnel largely from the regular army of each of its host nations, including its senior personnel, although it was also empowered to draft in scientific or medical help.

Story **The Mind Robber** ❀ Written by **Peter Ling** ❀ Featuring the **Second Doctor, Jamie and Zoe** ❀ Foe the **Master of the Land of Fiction** ❀ First broadcast **14 September–12 October 1968** ❀ **5 episodes**

Story **The Invasion** ❀ Written by **Derrick Sherwin, from a story by Kit Pedler** ❀ Featuring **the Second Doctor, Jamie, Zoe and UNIT** ❀ Foe the **Cybermen, Tobias Vaughn** ❀ First broadcast **2 November–21 December 1968** ❀ **8 episodes**

Story **The Krotons** ❀ Written by **Robert Holmes** ❀ Featuring **the Second Doctor, Jamie and Zoe** ❀ Foe the **Krotons** ❀ First broadcast **28 December 1968–18 January 1969** ❀ **4 episodes**

With a distinguished career as a regular soldier behind him, Lethbridge-Stewart was at first unprepared for the strange, inexplicable things that he would see as UNIT's commanding officer. He was equally unready for the Doctor's erratic, anarchic methods. The pair were thrust together again when the Time Lords exiled the Third Doctor to Earth, and he soon recognised the advantages to UNIT of recruiting the Doctor as his scientific adviser. But he could react equally quickly to the new Doctor's abrasive manner, and the two would often argue. As a military man, the Brigadier tended to favour a military solution as a first resort, which appalled the generally pacifist Doctor. An early but significant row centred on the Brigadier's decision to follow orders and blow up a Silurian base in Derbyshire while the Doctor was still hoping to broker peace.

Although he was unprepared for many of his alien encounters, the Brigadier was always willing to accept the evidence of his eyes.

Story **The Seeds of Death** ✤ Written by **Brian Hayles** ✤ Featuring **the Second Doctor, Jamie and Zoe** ✤ Foe **the Ice Warriors** ✤ First broadcast **25 January–1 March 1969** ✤ **6 episodes**

Story **The Space Pirates** ✤ Written by **Robert Holmes** ✤ Featuring **the Second Doctor, Jamie and Zoe** ✤ Foe **space pirates** ✤ First broadcast **8 March–12 April 1969** ✤ **6 episodes**

Story **The War Games** ✤ Written by **Terrance Dicks & Malcolm Hulke** ✤ Featuring **the Second Doctor, Jamie and Zoe** ✤ Foe **the War Lords** ✤ First broadcast **19 April–21 June 1969** ✤ **10 episodes**

Whether faced with marauding shop window dummies or an alien mind parasite, the Brigadier led his men from the front, never asking them to do anything that he wouldn't risk doing himself. He led the mission to recapture a prison from the Master, and risked his career to defy the UK government's representative in negotiations with the Axons.

The Brigadier remained firmly Earthbound, never becoming one of the Doctor's travelling companions. On one occasion, however, he was transported – along with three Doctors and the whole of UNIT HQ – into an antimatter universe. At first he thought they'd ended up on a beach at Cromer or, worse, in a foreign country. ('This could be construed as an invasion!')

Following his retirement to teach maths at a boys' school, Lethbridge-Stewart again found himself unwillingly leaving Earth for alien worlds and spaceships on a couple of occasions, even meeting an earlier version of himself and apparently suffering a nervous breakdown. But he remained on call, always ready to serve his country and protect his planet.

Story **Spearhead from Space** ✪ Written by **Robert Holmes** ✪ Featuring **the Third Doctor, Liz and UNIT** ✪ Foe **the Autons, the Nestene Consciousness** ✪ First broadcast **3–24 January 1970** ✪ **4 episodes**

Story **The Silurians** ✪ Written by **Malcolm Hulke** ✪ Featuring **the Third Doctor, Liz and UNIT** ✪ Foe **the Silurians** ✪ First broadcast **31 January– 14 March 1970** ✪ **7 episodes**

Story **The Ambassadors of Death** ✪ Written by **David Whitaker** ✪ Featuring **the Third Doctor, Liz and UNIT** ✪ Foe **General Carrington** ✪ First broadcast **21 March–2 May 1970** ✪ **7 episodes**

LIZ SHAW

Played by **Caroline John** First appearance **Spearhead from Space (1970)**
Last regular appearance **Inferno (1970)** Guest appearance **The Five Doctors (1983)**

Already a successful stage actress, Caroline John secured the part of Liz Shaw when she sent a photograph of herself in a bikini to several television producers. New producer Barry Letts interviewed her and cast her as Liz Shaw, but she stayed for only a year – Letts deciding that a clever scientist was not after all the ideal Doctor Who companion. She is married to Geoffrey Beevers, who went on to play the Master in 1981.

When the Third Doctor began his exile on Earth, Brigadier Lethbridge-Stewart had already decided to recruit a scientific adviser for UNIT. He drafted Professor Elizabeth Shaw in from Cambridge University since she had, he said, degrees in medicine, physics and 'a dozen other subjects'. Liz was reluctant to become involved and highly sceptical of the Brigadier's claims that he had repelled two previous invasions of Earth with the assistance of a mysterious genius.

The first Auton attack convinced her, and Liz assisted the Doctor for the next few months, until she decided that all he really needed was someone to pass him test tubes and tell him how brilliant he was.

PARALLEL EARTH

While UNIT was handling security for a top-secret drilling project, Liz and the Doctor were attempting to repair the TARDIS, which had been immobilised by the Time Lords. Leaching power from the Inferno project, the Doctor successfully activated the console and was propelled into a parallel universe.

Here, Britain had become a fascist state, peopled by militaristic counterparts of the Doctor's usual colleagues. Brigade-Leader Lethbridge-Stewart had him imprisoned as a spy, but the Doctor appealed to Section Leader Elizabeth Shaw's scientific background and persuaded her to help him escape.

Story **Inferno** ☻ Written by **Don Houghton** ☻ Featuring **the Third Doctor, Liz and UNIT** ☻ Foe **the Primords** ☻ First broadcast **9 May–20 June 1970** ☻ **7 episodes**

Story **Terror of the Autons** Written by **Robert Holmes** ☻ Featuring **the Third Doctor, Jo and UNIT** ☻ Foe **the Master, the Autons, the Nestene Consciousness** ☻ First broadcast **2–23 January 1971** ☻ **4 episodes**

Story **The Mind of Evil** ☻ Written by **Don Houghton** ☻ Featuring **the Third Doctor, Jo and UNIT** ☻ Foe **the Master, mind parasite** ☻ First broadcast **30 January–6 March 1971** ☻ **6 episodes**

SERGEANT BENTON

Played by **John Levene** First appearance **The Invasion (1968)**
Last appearance **The Android Invasion (1975)**

After a couple of stints inside monster costumes – as a Cyberman in The Moonbase and a Yeti in The Web of Fear – John Levene was cast as Benton for The Invasion. This Second Doctor story became the template for the early years of the Third Doctor's era, and, after a further fleeting appearance as a Yeti in The War Games, Levene's character returned to active duty for The Ambassadors of Death. Benton was part of the UNIT 'family' for the next five years. Corporal Benton was one of the earliest wave of Brigadier Lethbridge-Stewart's regular army recruits, who first met the Doctor during the attack on Earth by the Cybermen. Promoted to Sergeant and later Warrant Officer, Benton proved a dependable member of the Brigadier's HQ staff. He was liked and trusted by UNIT troops and always fought from the front as Earth faced a series of alien attacks. He also put his complete faith in the Doctor, and proved much readier than Lethbridge-Stewart to accept the simultaneous presence of three Doctors. He was equally unfazed by the interior dimensions of the TARDIS. Off-duty, Benton sometimes took his younger sister ballroom dancing, and he followed rugby. He retired from UNIT in 1979 to sell used cars.

Story **The Claws of Axos** ☻ Written by **Bob Baker & Dave Martin** ☻ Featuring **the Third Doctor, Jo and UNIT** ☻ Foe **the Master, the Axons** ☻ First broadcast **13 March–3 April 1971** ☻ **4 episodes**

Story **Colony in Space** ☻ Written by **Malcolm Hulke** ☻ Featuring **the Third Doctor, Jo and UNIT** ☻ Foe **the Master, IMC** ☻ First broadcast **10 April–15 May 1971** ☻ **6 episodes**

Story **The Daemons** ☻ Written by **Guy Leopold** ☻ Featuring **the Third Doctor, Jo and UNIT** ☻ Foe **the Master, Azal, Bok** ☻ First broadcast **22 May–19 June 1971** ☻ **5 episodes**

Story **Day of the Daleks** ☻ Written by **Louis Marks** ☻ Featuring **the Third Doctor, Jo and UNIT** ☻ Foe the **Daleks, the Ogrons** ☻ First broadcast **1–22 January 1972** ☻ **4 episodes**

Story **The Curse of Peladon** ☻ Written by **Brian Hayles** ☻ Featuring **the Third Doctor and Jo** ☻ Foe **Arcturus, Hepesh** ☻ First broadcast **29 January–19 February 1972** ☻ **4 episodes**

Story **The Sea Devils** ☻ Written by **Malcolm Hulke** ☻ Featuring **the Third Doctor and Jo** ☻ Foe **the Master, the Sea Devils** ☻ First broadcast **26 February–1 April 1972** ☻ **6 episodes**

MIKE YATES

Played by **Richard Franklin** First appearance **Terror of the Autons (1971)** Last regular appearance **Planet of the Spiders (1974)** Guest appearance **The Five Doctors (1983)**

Richard Franklin joined Doctor Who as **Captain Yates** after several years in popular television series like Crossroads, Dixon of Dock Green and The Saint. He was cast as both the Brigadier's number two and a potential romantic interest for new companion Jo, adding to the more action-orientated direction of the series during the Pertwee years.

Captain Michael Yates seemed the ideal officer to be UNIT's second in command – unflappable, efficient and on good terms with his men. But when he was hypnotised by the supercomputer BOSS and forced to work against his UNIT colleagues, Yates found his loyalties tested. Recovering from the experience, he was recruited by the secret organisation behind Operation Golden Age – a plan to roll back time and depopulate Earth. Discreetly dismissed from UNIT, he tried to make amends by alerting Sarah Jane Smith to events at a meditation centre involving the giant spiders of Metebelis Three.

ALPHA CENTAURI

Jo was expecting a night out with Mike Yates when the Doctor persuaded her to join him for a test flight in the TARDIS. They ended up on Peladon, a medieval planet about to join the Galactic Federation. Among the Federation representatives was the delegate from Alpha Centauri, a monocular hermaphrodite hexapod with a shrill voice and nervous disposition. Centauri remained on Peladon once the planet had joined the Federation, vouching for the Doctor when he later returned with Sarah Jane Smith.

JO GRANT

Played by **Katy Manning** First appearance **Terror of the Autons** (1971) Last appearance **The Green Death** (1973)

Having decided that a clever scientist was not the ideal companion for the Doctor, the production team devised a new assistant and selected 21-year-old Katy Manning for the part. Katy had previously had small roles in Softly, Softly: Taskforce and Man at the Top after training at the Webber Douglas Academy of Dramatic Art. She was extremely short-sighted and frequently blundered into the scenery or other actors, and a short scene in The Daemons was apparently inspired by her efforts to navigate for Jon Pertwee while holding a map upside down.

Story **The Mutants** ✆ Written by **Bob Baker & Dave Martin** ✆ Featuring **the Third Doctor and Jo** ✆ Foe **the Marshal** ✆ First broadcast **8 April–13 May 1972** ✆ **6 episodes**

Story **The Time Monster** ✆ Written by **Robert Sloman** ✆ Featuring **the Third Doctor, Jo and UNIT** ✆ Foe **the Master** ✆ First broadcast **20 May–24 June 1972** ✆ **6 episodes**

Story **The Three Doctors** ✆ Written by **Bob Baker & Dave Martin** ✆ Featuring **the First, Second and Third Doctors, Jo and UNIT** ✆ Foe **Omega, Gellguards** ✆ First broadcast **30 December 1972–20 January 1973** ✆ **4 episodes**

When a high-ranking UN official pulled some strings to secure his niece's appointment at UNIT, the Doctor was dismayed to learn that the clumsy young girl who had just ruined one of his experiments was to be his new assistant. He'd hoped that Liz Shaw's replacement would be another scientist, but Josephine Grant's qualifications stopped at General Science at A Level ('I didn't say I passed,' she told him later).

The Doctor soon warmed to Jo, however, quickly recognising that every setback made her more determined to succeed next time. On her first day at work, she was hypnotised by the Master and sent back to UNIT HQ with instructions to detonate a bomb, but soon afterwards she was rescuing the Doctor. Cheerful and resourceful, Jo was never happy to be kept out of the action, and

THE THREE DOCTORS

The Time Lords of Gallifrey owed their status to the solar engineer Omega, who had detonated a star to create the power source that fed their time-travel technology. Presumed lost, Omega had in fact been trapped in an antimatter universe on the other side of a black hole. Driven mad by his isolation, Omega plotted his revenge on the Time Lords and his return to our universe by draining Gallifrey's energy into the black hole. Breaking their own Laws of Time, the Time Lords brought together the Doctor's first three incarnations, who united to defeat Omega, assisted by Jo, the Brigadier and Sergeant Benton. The Brigadier had only reluctantly accepted that the Third Doctor was the same man as the stranger that had defeated the Yeti and the Cybermen, and was astounded to find himself facing three Doctors at once. Benton was more phlegmatic, and it was thanks to him and Jo that the Doctors stopped arguing for long enough to come up with a plan to defeat Omega.

Story **Carnival of Monsters** ☻ Written by **Robert Holmes** ☻ Featuring **the Third Doctor and Jo** ☻ Foe **Kalik, Drashigs** ☻ First broadcast **27 January–17 February 1973** ☻ **4 episodes**

Story **Frontier in Space** ☻ Written by **Malcolm Hulke** ☻ Featuring **the Third Doctor and Jo** ☻ Foe **the Master, the Ogrons, the Daleks** ☻ First broadcast **24 February–31 March 1973** ☻ **6 episodes**

Story **Planet of the Daleks** ☻ Written by **Terry Nation** ☻ Featuring **the Third Doctor and Jo** ☻ Foe **the Daleks** ☻ First broadcast **7 April–12 May 1973** ☻ **6 episodes**

frequently disobeyed orders to stay behind. As often as the Doctor rescued her from dangerous situations, she did the same for him. She was adept at picking locks and carried skeleton keys, which got them out of many a locked room.

The Doctor showed her new times and other worlds, and her instinct to speak her mind slowly grew into a self-confidence in her beliefs – after three years with the Doctor, she was prepared to forgo a trip to Metebelis Three and resign from UNIT in order to support Professor Jones's ecological group in Wales.

Story **The Green Death** ☺ Written by **Robert Sloman** ☺ Featuring **the Third Doctor, Jo and UNIT** ☺ Foe **BOSS, giant maggots** ☺ First broadcast **19 May–23 June 1973** ☺ **6 episodes**

Story **The Time Warrior** ☺ Written by **Robert Holmes** ☺ Featuring **the Third Doctor, Sarah Jane and UNIT** ☺ Foe **Linx the Sontaran** ☺ First broadcast **15 December 1973–5 January 1974** ☺ **4 episodes**

Story **Invasion of the Dinosaurs** ☺ Written by **Malcolm Hulke** ☺ Featuring **the Third Doctor, Sarah Jane and UNIT** ☺ Foe **dinosaurs** ☺ First broadcast **12 January–16 February 1974** ☺ **6 episodes**

PROFESSOR JONES

Clifford Jones was the youngest-ever winner of a Nobel Prize, a campaigner against pollution and a prominent advocate of renewable energy. He had set up a commune-cum-research centre in South Wales, known locally as the Nut Hutch, where he was attempting to develop an edible fungus as a replacement for meat. Nearby was Global Chemicals, whose chemical pollution in the disused local mines had caused maggots to mutate to giant size and become lethal. This threat dealt with, Cliff asked Jo to marry him and accompany him on a research trip to the Amazon and she finally left the Doctor.

Story **Death to the Daleks** ☻ Written by **Terry Nation** ☻
Featuring **the Third Doctor and Sarah Jane** ☻ Foe **the
Daleks, the Exxilons** ☻ First broadcast **23 February–16
March 1974** ☻ **4 episodes**

Story **The Monster of Peladon** ☻ Written by **Brian Hayles**
☻ Featuring **the Third Doctor and Sarah Jane** ☻ Foe **the
Ice Warriors** ☻ First broadcast **23 March–27 April 1974** ☻
6 episodes

Story **Planet of the Spiders** ☻ Written by **Robert Sloman**
☻ Featuring **the Third Doctor, Sarah Jane and UNIT** ☻
Foe **giant spiders** ☻ First broadcast **4 May–8 June 1974**
☻ **6 episodes**

SARAH JANE SMITH

Played by **Elisabeth Sladen** First appearance **The Time Warrior (1973)** Last regular
appearance **The Hand of Fear (1976)** Guest appearances **The Five Doctors (1983)**,
School Reunion (2006), **The Stolen Earth** and **Journey's End (2008)**

When Katy Manning left in 1973, the Doctor Who team realised that the series needed
to reflect significant changes in society at large. The next companion would be a more
independent and self-sufficient character. Elisabeth Sladen, who had already appeared
in Coronation Street, Z Cars, Doomwatch and several other programmes, was chosen
when she was recommended by a BBC producer. When she auditioned, Elisabeth gained
Jon Pertwee's immediate approval, which secured her a three-year stint as perhaps the
most popular companion, and the only one to have had her own spin-off show – twice. Twenty-five years after the first
broadcast of K-9 and Company (see page 45), Elisabeth returned to BBC One in The Sarah Jane Adventures.

Orphaned when she was three months old, Sarah Jane
Smith was raised by her aunt, Lavinia
Smith, a renowned virologist. Sarah
Jane was a strong-willed and
enthusiastic supporter of women's
rights, and became a journalist,
joining *Metropolitan* magazine by
the age of 23. Investigating the
disappearances of top scientists,
she infiltrated a secret research
centre. There she encountered
the Doctor, who she suspected
of kidnapping the scientists.

Hiding aboard the TARDIS, Sarah Jane was taken to medieval England, where a stranded Sontaran had been stealing the scientists from the future as he attempted to repair his spaceship. Eventually persuaded that the Doctor was one of the good guys, Sarah Jane joined him on his travels, and was with him when he regenerated.

As the Doctor recovered from his regeneration, Sarah Jane returned to her work as a freelance journalist, although she still made time to visit UNIT HQ to check on her friend's progress, taking the opportunity to ask the Brigadier to issue her with a UNIT pass to the National Institute for Advanced Scientific Research, known as Thinktank. So it was Sarah Jane who stumbled on Thinktank's scheme to arm robot K1 with a disintegrator gun and use it to steal operating codes for the world's atomic missiles. Although UNIT arrested the Thinktank director and the Doctor aborted the launch of the missiles, the robot decided to continue with the destruction of humanity. It had, however, responded to Sarah Jane's concern for its wellbeing, selecting her as the sole human survivor. Sarah Jane was upset when the Doctor was forced to destroy the robot, but took him up on his offer of another trip in the TARDIS, unexpectedly accompanied by UNIT's new medical officer.

Story **Robot** ✪ Written by **Terrance Dicks** ✪ Featuring **the Fourth Doctor, Sarah Jane, Harry and UNIT** ✪ Foe **Thinktank, giant robot** ✪ First broadcast **28 December 1974–18 January 1975** ✪ **4 episodes**

Story **The Ark in Space** ✪ Written by **Robert Holmes** ✪ Featuring **the Fourth Doctor, Sarah Jane and Harry** ✪ Foe **the Wirrn** ✪ First broadcast **25 January–15 February 1975** ✪ **4 episodes**

Story **The Sontaran Experiment** ✪ Written by **Bob Baker & Dave Martin** ✪ Featuring **the Fourth Doctor, Sarah Jane and Harry** ✪ Foe **the Sontarans** ✪ First broadcast **22 February–1 March 1975** ✪ **2 episodes**

HARRY SULLIVAN

Played by **Ian Marter** First appearance **Robot (1974)**
Last regular appearance **Terror of the Zygons (1975)** Guest appearance **The Android Invasion (1975)**

Having unsuccessfully auditioned for the part of Captain Yates, Ian Marter's first Doctor Who appearance was in 1973 as Lt. John Andrews in Carnival of Monsters. A year later, he was cast as Harry, a young action hero devised to complement a new and possibly older Doctor, before Tom Baker had been selected to replace Jon Pertwee. Marter left after a year, though he remained involved with Doctor Who until his death in 1986, writing several novelisations of television adventures.

The newly regenerated Doctor was placed in the care of UNIT's medical officer, Surgeon-Lieutenant Harry Sullivan, who soon found himself going undercover at Thinktank, being held hostage, and helping the Doctor develop a metal-eating virus to destroy a giant robot. But when Harry agreed to a 'little trip to the moon', he was astonished to be transported to a space station in the far future, where he helped the Doctor revive the cryogenically frozen survivors of solar flares that had devastated Earth. Nerva was under attack from the Wirrn, which planned to absorb the sleeping humans.

Harry was old-fashioned, always courteous to and concerned for 'the weaker sex' – he irritated Sarah Jane by continually calling her 'old thing' or 'old girl'. He was also rather clumsy, but brave, loyal and enthusiastic. Although the Doctor delighted in teasing him – once bellowing 'Harry Sullivan is an imbecile!' – Harry proved a dependable travelling companion. At one point, Harry believed that both his friends were dead and was about to take on a Sontaran with a wooden club when the Doctor stopped him. Loyal as he was, Harry took the first chance he had to keep his feet firmly on Earth, and left the TARDIS after the defeat of the Zygons.

Story **Genesis of the Daleks** ☺ Written by **Terry Nation** ☺ Featuring **the Fourth Doctor, Sarah Jane and Harry** ☺ Foe **Davros, the Daleks** ☺ First broadcast **8 March–12 April 1975** ☺ **6 episodes**

Story **Revenge of the Cybermen** ☺ Written by **Gerry Davis** ☺ Featuring **the Fourth Doctor, Sarah Jane and Harry** ☺ Foe **the Cybermen** ☺ First broadcast **19 April–10 May 1975** ☺ **4 episodes**

Story **Terror of the Zygons** ☺ Written by **Robert Banks Stewart** ☺ Featuring **the Fourth Doctor, Sarah Jane, Harry and UNIT** ☺ Foe **the Zygons, the Skarasen** ☺ First broadcast **30 August–20 September 1975** ☺ **4 episodes**

Best Friends

The Third Doctor had had a fatherly, protective relationship with Sarah Jane – one which she frequently reacted against, often ignoring his instructions and investigating on her own. But she and the new, younger-seeming Fourth Doctor had a more equal friendship, delighting in exploring time and space together. The Doctor was now less worried when Sarah Jane took the initiative, though he never lost his concern for her safety. And Sarah Jane's own devotion to her friend continued and increased. Her greatest fear, perhaps, was that he would go one step too far once too often, and she was distraught when she thought he had died – which happened with alarming regularity, as the Doctor narrowly escaped death at the hands of Ice Warriors, Sutekh or the Sisterhood of Karn. After a while, this even became a joke between them – 'You thought I was dead, didn't you?' the Doctor once commented. 'You're always making that mistake.'

This sort of banter was typical of their relationship. Aboard Space Station Nerva, Sarah Jane volunteered to crawl through narrow service ducts with a vital power cable, but she was on the point of giving up when the Doctor conned her into continuing by telling her that he had been wrong to think he could depend on a foolish girl. Only when she had managed to force herself through did she realise he had tricked her.

Sarah Jane shared the Doctor's instinctive desire to resist oppression and aggression. In her first adventure,

Story **Planet of Evil** ✺ Written by **Louis Marks** ✺ Featuring **the Fourth Doctor and Sarah Jane** ✺ Foe **antimatter monsters** ✺ First broadcast **27 September–18 October 1975** ✺ **4 episodes**

Story **Pyramids of Mars** ✺ Written by **Stephen Harris** ✺ Featuring **the Fourth Doctor and Sarah Jane** ✺ Foe **Sutekh, robot mummies** ✺ First broadcast **25 October–15 November 1975** ✺ **4 episodes**

Story **The Android Invasion** ✺ Written by **Terry Nation** ✺ Featuring **the Fourth Doctor, Sarah Jane, Harry and UNIT** ✺ Foe **the Kraals, androids** ✺ First broadcast **22 November–13 December 1975** ✺ **4 episodes**

she had rallied the despondent Sir Edward and persuaded him to resist the local baron Irongron, before leading a party to recapture the Doctor from Linx the Sontaran. On Skaro, she led a party of prisoners in an attempted breakout, and later tried to persuade the Doctor to complete his mission to destroy the Daleks before they were fully developed.

The Doctor once described Sarah Jane as his best friend and, if anyone had asked her, she would probably have said she would travel in the TARDIS for ever. But when the Doctor received a summons to Gallifrey, where non-Time Lords were forbidden, it marked the end of Sarah Jane's travels. The Doctor attempted to drop her off at her Croydon home – unfortunately, he missed by several hundred miles and left her in Aberdeen. Sarah Jane had to adjust to life back on Earth, incorrectly assuming that she would never see her best friend again…

Story **The Brain of Morbius** ☺ Written by **Robin Bland** ☺ Featuring **the Fourth Doctor and Sarah Jane** ☺ Foe **Morbius, Solon** ☺ First broadcast **3–24 January 1976** ☺ **4 episodes**

Story **The Seeds of Doom** ☺ Written by **Robert Banks Stewart** ☺ Featuring **the Fourth Doctor, Sarah Jane and UNIT** ☺ Foe **the Krynoids** ☺ First broadcast **31 January–6 March 1976** ☺ **6 episodes**

Story **The Masque of Mandragora** ☺ Written by **Louis Marks** ☺ Featuring **the Fourth Doctor and Sarah Jane** ☺ Foe **the Mandragora Helix** ☺ First broadcast **4–25 September 1976** ☺ **4 episodes**

LEELA

Played by **Louise Jameson**

First appearance **The Face of Evil (1977)** Last appearance **The Invasion of Time (1978)**

Continuing Doctor Who's tradition of featuring positive female companions like Sarah Jane, Liz, Zoe and Barbara, the production team decided to go a little further and devised a physically strong, savage character who could defend herself and the Doctor. Inspired by Eliza Doolittle in Shaw's Pygmalion, they also wanted someone the Doctor could teach. Louise Jameson was chosen from 60 auditioning actors.

Leela was a warrior of the tribe of Sevateem, the primitive descendents of a lost space expedition from Earth. Although she was highly intelligent and learned quickly, her knowledge and experience were very limited, and she had a

Story **The Hand of Fear** ⚙ Written by **Bob Baker & Dave Martin** ⚙ Featuring **the Fourth Doctor and Sarah Jane** ⚙ Foe **Eldrad** ⚙ First broadcast **2–23 October 1976** ⚙ **4 episodes**

Story **The Deadly Assassin** ⚙ Written by **Robert Holmes** ⚙ Featuring **the Fourth Doctor** ⚙ Foe **the Master** ⚙ First broadcast **30 October–20 November 1976** ⚙ **4 episodes**

Story **The Face of Evil** ⚙ Written by **Chris Boucher** ⚙ Featuring **the Fourth Doctor and Leela** ⚙ Foe **Xoanon** ⚙ First broadcast **1–22 January 1977** ⚙ **4 episodes**

JAGO AND LITEFOOT

During one of Leela's earliest educational trips with the Doctor – to a theatre in Victorian London – they discovered a 51st-century war criminal, Magnus Greel, was abducting young women and using their life forces to prolong his life. Attempting to stop Greel retrieving and activating his dangerously unstable time-travel device, the Doctor enlisted the help of the theatre owner Henry Jago and professor of pathology Gordon Litefoot. Litefoot bemusedly entertained Leela to supper at his home and later tried to explain the intricacies of taking tea. When the Doctor and Leela were both captured by Greel, Jago and Litefoot joined forces to track down and rescue their new friends, bravely confronting Greel's Chinese followers and the homicidal, knife-wielding mannequin Mr Sin.

simple, spontaneous approach to life. Reluctantly taking her aboard the TARDIS, the Doctor became something of a mentor to her, teaching her to read and write and to look for a scientific explanation rather than a magical one, and showing her the wonders of the universe and humanity's history. Most importantly, the Doctor taught her to value life.

Leela's first instinct had always been to fight, and she and the Doctor frequently clashed over her carrying a knife or poisonous Janis thorns. As the Doctor insisted, 'If people see you mean them no harm, they never hurt you. Nine times out of ten.' Leela felt that she was quickly proved right when they found themselves being attacked by killer robots on a Sandminer, battling a shape-shifting Rutan in a lighthouse on Fang Rock, and confronting murderous scientists who had been biologically influenced by an ancient and malevolent force known as the Fendahl. But her instinctive aggression was gradually tempered by the Doctor's influence and, by the time they faced the Usurians on the planet Pluto, she was using her knife to disable an attacker rather than to kill him.

Story **The Robots of Death** ✪ Written by **Chris Boucher** ✪ Featuring **the Fourth Doctor and Leela** ✪ Foe **Taren Capel, robots** ✪ First broadcast **29 January–19 February 1977** ✪ **4 episodes**

Story **The Talons of Weng-Chiang** ✪ Written by **Robert Holmes** ✪ Featuring **the Fourth Doctor and Leela** ✪ Foe **Magnus Greel, Mr Sin** ✪ First broadcast **26 February–2 April 1977** ✪ **6 episodes**

Story **Horror of Fang Rock** ✪ Written by **Terrance Dicks** ✪ Featuring **the Fourth Doctor and Leela** ✪ Foe **Rutan** ✪ First broadcast **3–24 September 1977** ✪ **4 episodes**

K-9

Voiced by **John Leeson** and **David Brierley** First appearance **The Invisible Enemy (1977)** Last appearance **Warriors' Gate (1981)** Guest appearances **The Five Doctors (1983)**, **School Reunion (2006)**, **Journey's End (2008)**

When writers Bob Baker and Dave Martin included a robot dog in their scripts for The Invisible Enemy, they had no idea what they were unleashing... The BBC's Visual Effects department constructed a working radio-controlled robot in a matter of weeks, and it was decided to keep K-9 on. He quickly became one of Doctor Who's most popular companions.

Medical complex the Bi-Al Foundation was built into an asteroid in the late 50th century, and among its senior staff was a specialist in extraterrestrial diseases, Professor Marius. On his appointment, Marius discovered that weight restrictions prevented him from taking his pet dog, so he constructed a talking mobile computer...

Story **The Invisible Enemy** ☻ Written by **Bob Baker & Dave Martin** ☻ Featuring **the Fourth Doctor, Leela and K-9 Mk I** ☻ Foe **the Nucleus of the Swarm** ☻ First broadcast **1–22 October 1977** ☻ **4 episodes**

Story **Image of the Fendahl** ☻ Written by **Chris Boucher** ☻ Featuring **the Fourth Doctor, Leela and K-9 Mk I** Foe **the Fendahl** ☻ First broadcast **29 October–19 November 1977** ☻ **4 episodes**

Story **The Sun Makers** ☻ Written by **Robert Holmes** ☻ Featuring **the Fourth Doctor, Leela and K-9 Mk I** ☻ Foe **the Usurians** ☻ First broadcast **26 November–17 December 1977** ☻ **4 episodes**

Story **Underworld** ☻ Written by **Bob Baker & Dave Martin** ☻ Featuring **the Fourth Doctor, Leela and K-9 Mk I** ☻ Foe **the Oracle, Seers** ☻ First broadcast **7–28 January 1978** ☻ **4 episodes**

Story **The Invasion of Time** ☻ Written by **David Agnew** ☻ Featuring **the Fourth Doctor, Leela and K-9 Mk I** ☻ Foe **the Vardans, the Sontarans** ☻ First broadcast **4 February–11 March 1978** ☻ **6 episodes**

When Leela took the Doctor – who had been infected by an alien virus – to Bi-Al, she was confronted by a querulous robot dog. K-9 had a vast information database, printout facilities, sensor ears with tracking capabilities, and a laser blaster fitted in his nose. Having helped the Doctor overcome the virus swarm, K-9 left Bi-Al in the TARDIS, taking the chance to expand his own knowledge to levels way beyond 50th-century Earth. The Doctor quickly came to regard the robot dog as his second-best friend. He trusted K-9 alone with details of his plan to lure the Vardans into a trap by pretending to assist them in an invasion of Gallifrey – a plan he kept secret even from Leela. The Vardans themselves, however, were a front for the Sontarans, who invaded Gallifrey in force.

When K-9 chose to stay on Gallifrey with Leela, the Doctor built himself a replacement robot dog. Like his predecessor, K-9 Mark II could beat the Doctor at chess and often took instructions quite literally – he erased his own memory of tennis when told to

THE LORDS OF TIME

Although the Doctor considered his own people dull and uninteresting – even thinking that the Vardan takeover might do them some good – he usually found plenty of willing support among the Time Lords. Castellan Spandrell and Coordinator Engin helped him defeat the Master on one visit, and he was only able to repel the Vardan and Sontaran invasions with the help of Rodan, Chancellor Borusa, and Andred, Commander of the Chancellery Guard. Alongside Leela, Andred led a small force of Time Lords and Outsiders (who had previously rejected Time Lord society) against the Sontarans. Leela fell in love with Andred and she and K-9 decided to remain on Gallifrey.

Story **The Ribos Operation** ☺ Written by **Robert Holmes** ☺ Featuring **the Fourth Doctor, Romana I and K-9 Mk II** ☺ Foe **Graff Vynda-K** ☺ First broadcast **2–23 September 1978** ☺ **4 episodes**

Story **The Pirate Planet** ☺ Written by **Douglas Adams** ☺ Featuring **the Fourth Doctor, Romana I and K-9 Mk II** ☺ Foe **Xanxia, the Captain** ☺ First broadcast **30 September–21 October 1978** ☺ **4 episodes**

Story **The Stones of Blood** ☺ Written by **David Fisher** ☺ Featuring **the Fourth Doctor, Romana I and K-9 Mk II** ☺ Foe **the Ogri, Cessair of Diplos** ☺ First broadcast **28 October–18 November 1978** ☺ **4 episodes**

'forget it'. But this new, improved version could also respond to signals from a dog whistle, track and analyse the psychic traces of telepaths, and self-regenerate with assistance from the TARDIS. He also held complete plans for the TARDIS systems in his database. His time on the TARDIS came to an end when he was ravaged by time winds – only able to function in E-Space, he stayed there with Romana.

The Doctor also built a third K-9, as a gift for Sarah Jane Smith…

THE WHITE GUARDIAN

The Guardians were all-powerful beings existing outside and beyond normal time and space. Judging that the universe had reached a point where the balance between good and evil needed to be restored, the White Guardian – the Guardian of Light and Time – selected the Doctor to locate the six disguised segments of the Key to Time before the universe was plunged into eternal chaos. When reassembled, the Key would stop everything for a single moment and the universal balance would be restored. The White Guardian warned the Doctor that there was a Guardian of Darkness and Chaos – the Black Guardian – who also wanted the Key. The Doctor's successful completion of his mission was to earn him the undying enmity of the Black Guardian, and the White Guardian would later attempt to warn the Fifth Doctor of the threat. But first the Fourth Doctor had to find the segments, and to do that he would need a new companion…

⬡ ROMANA I

Played by **Mary Tamm**
First appearance **The Ribos Operation (1978)** Last appearance **The Armageddon Factor (1979)**

New producer Graham Williams decided that his second season would show the Doctor undertaking an epic quest for the Key to Time on behalf of an omnipotent being superior to the Time Lords, aided by a young Time Lady – an 'ice princess', whose reserve and technical prowess would contrast with the savagery of Leela. Mary Tamm, a drama school contemporary and friend of Louise Jameson's, accepted the role, partly because the beautiful intellectual seemed a fresh direction for a Doctor Who companion.

Romanadvoratrelundar was a recent graduate from the Time Lord Academy, academically gifted – she attained a triple first – but naive and inexperienced. She believed she had been sent on her mission by the Time Lord President, though this was in fact the disguised White Guardian, and she quickly found that the Doctor resented having her foisted upon him. At 125 (but claiming to be nearly 140), she had not previously left Gallifrey so was unprepared for the realities of time and space travel. But Romana learned quickly as she travelled, winning the Doctor over while teasing him about her superior academic qualifications.

Story **The Androids of Tara** ⬡ Written by **David Fisher** ⬡ Featuring **the Fourth Doctor, Romana I and K-9 Mk II** ⬡ Foe **Count Grendel** ⬡ First broadcast **25 November–16 December 1978** ⬡ 4 episodes

Story **The Power of Kroll** ⬡ Written by **Robert Holmes** ⬡ Featuring **the Fourth Doctor and Romana I** ⬡ Foe **Kroll** ⬡ First broadcast **23 December 1978–13 January 1979** ⬡ 4 episodes

Story **The Armageddon Factor** ⬡ Written by **Bob Baker & Dave Martin** ⬡ Featuring **the Fourth Doctor, Romana I and K-9 Mk II** ⬡ Foe **the Black Guardian, the Shadow** ⬡ First broadcast **20 January–24 February 1979** ⬡ 6 episodes

⬡ ROMANA II

Played by **Lalla Ward** First appearance **Destiny of the Daleks (1979)**
Last appearance **Warriors' Gate (1981)** Guest appearance **The Five Doctors (1983)**

Mary Tamm left after just one season, but Graham Williams decided to retain the character of Romana. The final segment of the Key to Time had been disguised as Princess Astra of Atrios, played by Lalla Ward. She

had got on well with Tom Baker during filming of The Armageddon Factor, so the 17th season began with Romana regenerating into a copy of Astra. Faced with a companion wearing someone else's body, the Doctor initially told Romana to have another go, and she tried out three other forms before settling again on Astra's. The new Romana was more light-hearted and adventurous, perhaps influenced by the Doctor's own brash confidence, and, though she kept a keen sense of her own superiority, she was less severe and cold. From now on, the Doctor and Romana operated as a team of equals, still sparring and teasing each other, but rarely falling out.

Story **Destiny of the Daleks** ⊛ Written by **Terry Nation** ⊛ Featuring **the Fourth Doctor, Romana II and K-9 Mk II** ⊛ Foe **Davros, the Daleks, the Movellans** ⊛ First broadcast **1–22 September 1979** ⊛ 4 episodes

Story **City of Death** ⊛ Written by **David Agnew** ⊛ Featuring **the Fourth Doctor and Romana II** ⊛ Foe **Scaroth** ⊛ First broadcast **29 September–20 October 1979** ⊛ 4 episodes

Story **The Creature from the Pit** ⊛ Written by **David Fisher** ⊛ Featuring **the Fourth Doctor, Romana II and K-9 Mk II** ⊛ Foe **Adrasta** ⊛ First broadcast **27 October–17 November 1979** ⊛ 4 episodes

DUGGAN

The Doctor and Romana's Paris break was interrupted by Scaroth, last of the Jagaroth, who was funding time-travel experiments by selling stolen artworks. He wanted to go back 400 million years and stop the destruction of his spaceship, the event that had sparked the creation of all life on Earth. Scaroth's activities were being investigated by a private detective, Duggan, who travelled back in time with the Doctor and Romana. Duggan knocked Scaroth out before he could reach his ship – the most important punch in history.

Where the first Romana's technical expertise tended to be theoretical, the second shared the Doctor's aptitude for inventive solutions to practical problems. She constructed her own sonic screwdriver – probably a better model, since the Doctor tried to pocket it – and devised workable time-travel devices in Paris and on Argolis.

Romana's travels with the Doctor also convinced her that he was right to reject Time Lord principles of non-interference, and the two gleefully set about defeating Daleks and Movellans, liberating Nimon slaves and destroying vampires. When the Time Lords summoned her home, she realised that her new outlook meant that she would no longer fit in on Gallifrey. She chose to leave the TARDIS and stay in E-Space, helping a race of time-sensitive Tharils escape enslavement.

Story **Nightmare of Eden** ☻ Written by **Bob Baker** ☻ Featuring **the Fourth Doctor, Romana II and K-9 Mk II** ☻ Foe **the Mandrels** ☻ First broadcast **24 November–15 December 1979** ☻ **4 episodes**

Story **The Horns of Nimon** ☻ Written by **Anthony Read** ☻ Featuring **the Fourth Doctor, Romana II and K-9 Mk II** ☻ Foe **the Nimon** ☻ First broadcast **22 December 1979–12 January 1980** ☻ **4 episodes**

Story **The Leisure Hive** ☻ Written by **David Fisher** ☻ Featuring **the Fourth Doctor, Romana II and K-9 Mk II** ☻ Foe **the Foamasi** ☻ First broadcast **30 August–20 September 1980** ☻ **4 episodes**

ADRIC

Played by **Matthew Waterhouse** First appearance **Full Circle** (1980) Last appearance **Earthshock** (1982) Guest appearances **Time-Flight** (1982), The Caves of Androzani (1984)

Nineteen-year-old Matthew Waterhouse was the first 'fan' of the series to be cast as a Doctor Who regular – a year before, he had even had a letter published in Doctor Who Weekly. He had recently appeared in To Serve Them All My Days and was chosen to play an 'Artful Dodger' character.

When the TARDIS slipped through a portal from our 'N-Space' into the smaller universe of 'E-Space', the Doctor and Romana found themselves on the planet Alzarius. Here they met Adric, a rebellious teenager with a gift for mathematics and a tendency to sulk if he didn't get his own way.

The Alzarians believed they were descended from the survivors of a crashed starliner but were in fact subject to a process of accelerated evolution from the planet's native Marshmen. They had developed a rigidly defined society geared entirely to repairing the

Story **Meglos** ✦ Written by **John Flanagan & Andrew McCulloch** ✦ Featuring **the Fourth Doctor, Romana II and K-9 Mk II** ✦ Foe **Meglos** ✦ First broadcast 27 September–18 October 1980 ✦ 4 episodes

Story **Full Circle** ✦ Written by **Andrew Smith** ✦ Featuring **the Fourth Doctor, Romana II, Adric and K-9 Mk II** ✦ Foe **Marshmen** ✦ First broadcast 25 October–15 November 1980 ✦ 4 episodes

Story **State of Decay** ✦ Written by **Terrance Dicks** ✦ Featuring **the Fourth Doctor, Romana II, Adric and K-9 Mk II** ✦ Foe **vampires** ✦ First broadcast 22 November–13 December 1980 ✦ 4 episodes

THE FOURTH DOCTOR

K-9 AND COMPANY

Story **A Girl's Best Friend** ☻ Written by **Terence Dudley** ☻ Featuring **Sarah Jane and K-9 Mk III** ☻ First broadcast **28 December 1981** ☻ **1 episode**

Doctor Who's first spin-off brought the show's two most popular companions back to our screens…
Staying at her aunt Lavinia Smith's house for Christmas, Sarah Jane Smith discovered that the Doctor had not forgotten her. Waiting for her was an unexpected gift – K-9 Mark III. Together, Sarah Jane and K-9 unmasked a black magic coven.

K-9 stayed with Sarah Jane for many years, but time took its toll and the robot began to rust and malfunction. There was no way for Sarah Jane to repair him and, by 2007, he had broken down completely…

Starliner and escaping the planet, but Adric was a would-be member of a small band of rebels against this system. Stowing away aboard the TARDIS, Adric retained his rebellious streak: he often acted impulsively against the Doctor's orders, was happy to steal whatever he wanted, and seemed quite easily won over by promises of power.

After the Doctor regenerated, Adric had frequent arguments with him and with their new companions. Adric sometimes felt that Nyssa, Tegan and the new Doctor treated him like a child, and eventually declared that he wanted to leave the TARDIS and return to E-Space. He plotted a course, but admitted that, in truth, he wanted to stay. Ultimately, however, he sacrificed his life to save Earth from the Cybermen.

Story **Warriors' Gate** ☻ Written by **Steve Gallagher** ☻ Featuring **the Fourth Doctor, Romana II, Adric and K-9 Mk II** ☻ Foe **slave traders** ☻ First broadcast **3–24 January 1981** ☻ **4 episodes**

Story **The Keeper of Traken** ☻ Written by **Johnny Byrne** ☻ Featuring **the Fourth Doctor, Adric and Nyssa** ☻ Foe **the Master** ☻ First broadcast **31 January–21 February 1981** ☻ **4 episodes**

Story **Logopolis** ☻ Written by **Christopher H. Bidmead** ☻ Featuring **the Fourth Doctor, Adric, Nyssa and Tegan** ☻ Foe **the Master** ☻ First broadcast **28 February–21 March 1981** ☻ **4 episodes**

NYSSA

Played by **Sarah Sutton** First appearance **The Keeper of Traken** (1981) Last appearance **Terminus** (1983) Guest appearance **The Caves of Androzani** (1984)

Story **Castrovalva** ☺ Written by **Christopher H. Bidmead** ☺ Featuring **the Fifth Doctor, Adric, Nyssa and Tegan** ☺ Foe **the Master** ☺ First broadcast **4–12 January 1982** ☺ **4 episodes**

Story **Four to Doomsday** ☺ Written by **Terence Dudley** ☺ Featuring **the Fifth Doctor, Adric, Nyssa and Tegan** ☺ Foe **Monarch** ☺ First broadcast **18–26 January 1982** ☺ **4 episodes**

As the Tom Baker era drew to a close, producer John Nathan-Turner briefly considered bringing back an old companion to smooth the transition. Instead, Peter Davison's Doctor was joined by three new companions, although Nyssa of Traken was originally created for just one Fourth Doctor story. But Sarah Sutton impressed Nathan-Turner during rehearsals, so she was contracted to remain on the series.

Nyssa was the daughter of Tremas, one of the ruling Consuls of the Union of Traken. After a failed attempt to take over Traken, the Master stole Tremas's body, leaving Nyssa orphaned. She contacted the TARDIS, but the Master now had a new scheme, which almost ended the universe, in the process destroying Traken and causing the Doctor to regenerate.

Practical and logical, Nyssa was an accomplished scientist. She shared the new Doctor's enthusiasm for the technology they discovered aboard an Urbankan

spaceship, and constructed a sonic booster to fight off an android when the TARDIS took them to 17th-century England, where they encountered a group of Terileptils planning to wipe out humanity. Nyssa, however, suffered a series of losses during her time in the TARDIS: the deaths of her father, stepmother and home world were followed by Adric's sacrifice, and she had to witness the Doctor's apparent execution by the Time Lords. When the TARDIS arrived on Terminus, a 'hospital' for victims of Lazar's Disease, she decided to stay there, at last finding a practical way in which she could use her technical skills to help others.

RICHARD MACE

Landing in England in 1666, the Doctor and his friends soon stumbled across Richard Mace, an amiable out-of-work thespian and would-be highwayman. Mace's primary aim was to keep himself alive, well and comfortable, and he happily helped himself to food and wine wherever he found them. But he was persuaded to help fight the Terileptils, despite his constant bewilderment at the inexplicably strange things he was seeing and hearing.

During the final battle with the Terileptils, an exploding gun started the Great Fire of London, and Mace turned down the Doctor's offer of a trip in the TARDIS, instead staying to help fight the fire.

Story **Kinda** ☻ Written by **Christopher Bailey** ☻ Featuring **the Fifth Doctor, Adric, Nyssa and Tegan** ☻ Foe **the Mara** ☻ First broadcast **1–9 February 1982** ☻ **4 episodes**

Story **The Visitation** ☺ Written by **Eric Saward** ☺ Featuring **the Fifth Doctor, Adric, Nyssa and Tegan** ☺ Foe **Terileptils** ☺ First broadcast **15–23 February 1982** ☺ **4 episodes**

Story **Black Orchid** ☺ Written by **Terence Dudley** ☺ Featuring **the Fifth Doctor, Adric, Nyssa and Tegan** ☺ First broadcast **1–2 March 1982** ☺ **2 episodes**

TEGAN JOVANKA

Played by **Janet Fielding** First appearance **Logopolis (1981)** Last appearance **Resurrection of the Daleks (1984)** Guest appearance **The Caves of Androzani (1984)**

Hoping to extend Doctor Who's sales abroad, John Nathan-Turner drew up plans for an Australian companion. Among the actresses auditioning for the part was 23-year-old Janet Fielding, who gave a strong performance but was shorter than the minimum height requirement for an air hostess at the time. She persuaded Nathan-Turner that Australian regulations were different, and was given the role, staying on for almost the whole Peter Davison era.

Tegan Jovanka was on her way to her first day's work as an air stewardess when, stopping to repair a flat tyre, her curiosity led her into the TARDIS during the Fourth Doctor's final battle with the Master. She suddenly found herself carried off to alien worlds like Logopolis, Castrovalva and Deva-Loka and to Earth decades or centuries before she was born. Naturally quick-tempered and bossy, she described herself as 'a mouth on legs', though the Doctor saw her as a 'coordinator', holding the TARDIS crew together.

Story **Earthshock** ⊚ Written by **Eric Saward** ⊚ Featuring the Fifth Doctor, Adric, Nyssa and Tegan ⊚ Foe the Cybermen ⊚ First broadcast **8–16 March 1982** ⊚ **4 episodes**

Story **Time-Flight** ⊚ Written by **Peter Grimwade** ⊚ Featuring the Fifth Doctor, Nyssa and Tegan ⊚ Foe the Master, the Plasmatons, the Xeraphin ⊚ First broadcast **22–30 March 1982** ⊚ **4 episodes**

Story **Arc of Infinity** ⊚ Written by **Johnny Byrne** ⊚ Featuring the Fifth Doctor, Nyssa and Tegan ⊚ Foe Omega, the Ergon ⊚ First broadcast **3–12 January 1983** ⊚ **4 episodes**

After Adric's death, the Doctor perhaps assumed that Tegan would be happy to return home, and he left her at Heathrow. Their paths soon crossed again, however, when Tegan was captured by renegade Time Lord Omega during his attempt to leave his antimatter universe through the Arc of Infinity. Once the Doctor had banished Omega using a matter converter, Tegan rejoined the TARDIS crew.

On the planet Deva-Loka, Tegan was possessed by an ancient and malign intelligence. The Mara was defeated, but it kept a hold on her and later directed her to take the TARDIS to the planet Manussa, where the Mara could regain corporeal form. As the Mara's influence grew, Tegan began to merge with it, but the Doctor helped her to resist it. When Tegan reasserted her own will, the Mara's physical form – a giant snake – was once again expelled.

After an encounter with the Daleks, Tegan decided she was no longer enjoying her travels with the Doctor – she had witnessed too many deaths and it had stopped being fun.

THE BRIGADIER (RETIRED)

John Nathan-Turner decided to mark Doctor Who's 20th anniversary with a season in which every story featured at least one returning character from the series' past. The third adventure, Mawdryn Undead, brought back both the Guardians from the Key to Time season, plus one of the Doctor's oldest friends. Nicholas Courtney had not appeared since 1975's Terror of the Zygons, but he now returned to play two versions of the Brigadier.

Brigadier Lethbridge-Stewart left UNIT in 1976, retiring to teach maths at a boys' school. In 1977, he suffered a nervous breakdown and, when the Doctor met him in 1983, he had no memory of the Time Lord, though he still remembered his other former UNIT colleagues. The 1977 Brigadier had in fact met his older self aboard an orbiting spaceship. The resultant time differential short-out knocked out the younger Brigadier, causing his memory loss and breakdown. The Doctor returned the Brigadiers to their own times. Later in 1983, Lethbridge-Stewart attended a UNIT reunion, a chance to re-meet more old friends than he'd ever expected.

Story **Snakedance** ☼ Written by **Christopher Bailey** ☼ Featuring **the Fifth Doctor, Nyssa and Tegan** ☼ Foe **the Mara** ☼ First broadcast **18–26 January 1983** ☼ **4 episodes**

Story **Mawdryn Undead** ☼ Written by **Peter Grimwade** ☼ Featuring **the Fifth Doctor, Nyssa, Tegan, Turlough and the Brigadier** ☼ Foe **the Black Guardian** ☼ First broadcast **1–9 February 1983** ☼ **4 episodes**

Story **Terminus** ☼ Written by **Steve Gallagher** ☼ Featuring **the Fifth Doctor, Nyssa, Tegan and Turlough** ☼ Foe **the Black Guardian, the Vanir** ☼ First broadcast **15–20 February 1983** ☼ **4 episodes**

THE FIVE DOCTORS

Doctor Who's 20th-birthday celebrations culminated in an ambitious 90-minute special broadcast during the show's anniversary week. It was written by long-time writer and former script editor Terrance Dicks, whose brief was to include all five Doctors and as many companions and monsters as possible. Current Doctor Peter Davison was joined by Patrick Troughton and Jon Pertwee, and the late William Hartnell was replaced by Richard Hurndall, while Tom Baker was represented by previously unscreened footage from an abandoned story called Shada. Borusa, President of the Time Lords, hoped to find Rassilon's secret

of immortality. Using a Time Scoop, he deposited the Doctors inside the Death Zone on Gallifrey, with friends to help them and old enemies to fight. Though the Fourth Doctor and Romana were trapped in a time eddy, the First Doctor and Susan, the Second Doctor and the Brigadier, the Third Doctor and Sarah Jane, and the Fifth Doctor, Tegan and Turlough all made their way past a Dalek, a Yeti, Cybermen, a Raston Warrior Robot and the Master – as well as illusory images of Jamie, Zoe, Liz Shaw and Mike Yates – to the tomb of Rassilon in the Dark Tower.

Story **Enlightenment** ☺ Written by **Barbara Clegg** ☺ Featuring **the Fifth Doctor, Tegan and Turlough** ☺ Foe **the Black Guardian, the Eternals** ☺ First broadcast **1–9 March 1983** ☺ 4 episodes

Story **The King's Demons** ☺ Written by **Terence Dudley** ☺ Featuring **the Fifth Doctor, Tegan and Turlough** ☺ Foe **the Master** ☺ First broadcast **15–16 March 1983** ☺ 2 episodes

Story **The Five Doctors** ☺ Written by **Terrance Dicks** ☺ Featuring **the Doctors, Tegan, Turlough, the Brigadier, Sarah Jane, K-9 Mk III, Romana II, Susan, Liz, Mike Yates, Jamie and Zoe** ☺ Foe **Dalek, Yeti, Cybermen, Raston Warrior Robot, the Master, Borusa** ☺ First UK broadcast **25 November 1983** ☺ 1 episode

VISLOR TURLOUGH

Played by **Mark Strickson** First appearance **Mawdryn Undead (1983)** Last appearance **Planet of Fire (1984)**
Guest appearance **The Caves of Androzani (1984)**

John Nathan-Turner and script editor Eric Saward were hoping to inject some danger into the
new companion, making him an untrustworthy alien on a mission to kill the Doctor. Mark
Strickson was playing an ambulance driver on BBC soap Angels and had been
offered a regular role on that when he accepted the part of Turlough. It was felt
that he too closely resembled Peter Davison, so his hair and eyebrows were dyed
red, which fortuitously helped to emphasise Turlough's non-terrestrial origins.

Exiled from the planet Trion and stranded on Earth,
Turlough dreamed of returning home, which he
ultimately did when offered the chance. But
he was trapped in a boys' public school when
he was recruited by the Black Guardian to
assassinate the Doctor. Opportunistic as he
was, Turlough was not a killer, and he made

Story **Warriors of the Deep** ☺ Written by
Johnny Byrne ☺ Featuring **the Fifth Doctor,
Tegan and Turlough** ☺ Foe **the Silurians, the
Sea Devils, the Myrka** ☺ First broadcast **5–13
January 1984** ☺ **4 episodes**

Story **The Awakening** ☺ Written by **Eric Pringle** ☺
Featuring **the Fifth Doctor, Tegan and Turlough**
☺ Foe **the Malus** ☺ First broadcast **19–20 January
1984** ☺ **2 episodes**

Story **Frontios** ☺ Written by **Christopher H.
Bidmead** ☺ Featuring **the Fifth Doctor, Tegan
and Turlough** ☺ Foe **Tractators** ☺ First broadcast
26 January–3 February 1984 ☺ **4 episodes**

only half-hearted, unsuccessful attempts to complete his mission. Though suspicious of him, the Doctor welcomed him aboard the TARDIS, an act that eventually spurred Turlough to reject the Black Guardian. As a member of a spacefaring race, Turlough was technologically adept and understood the basics of how the TARDIS operated. He was also short-tempered and secretive, and Tegan's doubts about him lingered long after the Doctor had accepted him. His well-developed instinct for self-preservation meant he usually steered clear of danger, although he was responsible for saving Peri Brown and bringing her aboard the TARDIS…

Story **Resurrection of the Daleks** ☻ Written by **Eric Saward** ☻ Featuring the **Fifth Doctor, Tegan and Turlough** ☻ Foe **Davros, the Daleks** ☻ First broadcast **8–15 February 1984** ☻ **2 episodes**

Story **Planet of Fire** ☻ Written by **Peter Grimwade** ☻ Featuring the **Fifth Doctor, Turlough and Peri** ☻ Foe **the Master** ☻ First broadcast **23 February–2 March 1984** ☻ **4 episodes**

Story **The Caves of Androzani** ☻ Written by **Robert Holmes** ☻ Featuring **the Fifth Doctor and Peri** ☻ Foe **Sharaz Jek, Morgus** ☻ First broadcast **8–16 March 1984** ☻ **4 episodes**

KAMELION

John Nathan-Turner was impressed when an Oxford-based computer company demonstrated a functioning humanoid robot and decided to introduce it at the end of Season 20. Technical problems, however, made the robot rather unreliable and, with studio time always tight, Kamelion's first story, The King's Demons, introduced him as a shape-changing android, allowing other actors to portray him at various stages in the story. Gerald Flood provided Kamelion's default voice and returned in Season 21 for an untransmitted scene in The Awakening and a farewell story, Planet of Fire.

The Doctor discovered the Master had disguised Kamelion as King John, hoping to prevent Magna Carta being signed in 1215. The android was controlled by psychokinetics and was highly susceptible to stronger wills. The Doctor was able to wrest control from the Master and took Kamelion aboard the TARDIS, but the Master retained a perpetual mental link with him. Realising this, Kamelion begged to be destroyed.

PERI BROWN

Played by **Nicola Bryant**
First appearance **Planet of Fire (1984)**
Last appearance **The Trial of a Time Lord (1986)**

With Janet Fielding's Tegan bowing out after three years, John Nathan-Turner wanted another non-British companion, this time hoping to appeal to the growing US market by incorporating an American character. Nicola Bryant was actually from Surrey in southern England, but her assumed accent was good enough to fool cast, crew and press.

Perpugilliam Brown, known as Peri, was a 19-year-old botany student from the United States of America. Bored during a family holiday in Lanzarote that had turned out to be an archaeological field trip and marooned on her stepfather's boat, she ended up nearly drowning. She was rescued by Turlough and taken aboard the TARDIS. Despite getting caught up in a battle with the Master on the volcano-ravaged planet Sarn, Peri asked to stay on and travel with the Doctor. They quickly developed a close friendship, though this was soon threatened by the Doctor's regeneration.

Story **The Twin Dilemma** ⊕ Written by **Anthony Steven** ⊕ Featuring **the Sixth Doctor and Peri** ⊕ Foe **Mestor** ⊕ First broadcast **22–30 March 1984** ⊕ **4 episodes**

Story **Attack of the Cybermen** ⊕ Written by **Paula Moore** ⊕ Featuring **the Sixth Doctor and Peri** ⊕ Foe **the Cybermen** ⊕ First broadcast **5–12 January 1985** ⊕ **2 episodes**

Story **Vengeance on Varos** ⊕ Written by **Philip Martin** ⊕ Featuring **the Sixth Doctor and Peri** ⊕ Foe **Sil** ⊕ First broadcast **19–26 January 1985** ⊕ **2 episodes**

Visiting Androzani Minor, both Peri and the Doctor contracted spectrox toxaemia. The Doctor managed to procure an antidote, but only enough for one, and he sacrificed his life to save Peri's. Peri was bewildered and frightened to see her new friend change into his sixth persona, and terrified when post-regenerative trauma made him abusive, insulting and violent towards her. Although she remained loyal to him, their relationship changed from good-natured teasing to continual arguing, and it took a long time before Peri and the Sixth Doctor really enjoyed each other's company. Ironically, by the time this happened, they were on the verge of an enforced parting of the ways.

During her travels, Peri often found herself an object of desire for various male admirers. On Androzani Minor, Sharaz Jek was infatuated with her, wanting to feast his eyes on her beauty for ever; the mutant Borad on the planet Karfel planned to make her his consort; mortician Jobel at Tranquil Repose hoped to seduce her; and on Ravalox

Story **The Mark of the Rani** ✪ Written by **Pip and Jane Baker** ✪ Featuring **the Sixth Doctor and Peri** ✪ Foe **the Master, the Rani** ✪ First broadcast **2–9 February 1985** ✪ **2 episodes**

Story **The Two Doctors** ✪ Written by **Robert Holmes** ✪ Featuring **the Sixth and Second Doctors, Peri and Jamie** ✪ Foe **the Sontarans, the Androgums** ✪ First broadcast **16 February–2 March 1985** ✪ **3 episodes**

Story **Timelash** ✪ Written by **Glen McCoy** ✪ Featuring **the Sixth Doctor and Peri** ✪ Foe **the Borad** ✪ First broadcast **9–16 March 1985** ✪ **2 episodes**

THE SECOND DOCTOR AND JAMIE MACRIMMON

Fraser Hines had been able to make only a cameo appearance in The Five Doctors, but he and Patrick Troughton were both keen to make another return. A story was specially commissioned from Robert Holmes that would assemble two Doctors, two companions and the Sontarans in space and Spain.

When the Second Doctor and Jamie were caught in a raid on a space station, the Sixth Doctor collapsed as his earlier self was, apparently, executed. Jamie survived the attack and united with the Doctor and Peri to find 'his' Doctor. The trail led to Spain, where a corrupt scientist, two Androgums and members of the Ninth Sontaran Battle Group planned to use the Doctor to activate a time-travel device.

she faced the prospect of arranged marriages with multiple husbands. The Mentor Sil was rare in finding her human form disgusting, and he attempted to turn her into a bird creature on Varos. When the Doctor and Peri encountered him again, on his home planet of Thoros-Beta, Sil welcomed her as 'the repulsive one', though the imprisoned warrior king of the Krontep, Yrcanos was more enamoured of her. But, with his mind affected by an interrogation machine, the Doctor betrayed and abandoned Peri, and her body was selected as the receptacle for the brain of the Mentor leader, Kiv. The Doctor was snatched from Thoros-Beta by the Time Lords to face trial before he could save Peri. It seemed that

the mind transfer had been successful and Kiv/Peri had died during a suicidal assault by Yrcanos. This was, however, later revealed to be a fiction devised by the Valeyard – in fact both Peri and Yrcanos had survived and, with the Doctor gone, the warlord had made Peri a warrior queen on his home world.

Story **Revelation of the Daleks** ☻ Written by **Eric Saward** ☻ Featuring **the Sixth Doctor and Peri** ☻ Foe **Davros, the Daleks** ☻ First broadcast **23–30 March 1985** ☻ **2 episodes**

Story **The Trial of a Time Lord** ☻ Written by **Robert Holmes, Philip Martin and Pip & June Baker** ☻ Featuring **the Sixth Doctor, Peri and Mel** ☻ Foe **Drathro, the Mentors, the Vervoids, the Master, the Valeyard** ☻ First broadcast **6 September–6 December 1986** ☻ **14 episodes**

MELANIE BUSH

Played by **Bonnie Langford**
First appearance **The Trial of a Time Lord (1986)** Last appearance **Dragonfire (1987)**

When John Nathan-Turner decided to replace Peri with a red-haired fitness fanatic, he thought that popular entertainer Bonnie Langford would be ideal for the role. A singer and dancer, she had been a child actor in Just William ten years earlier.

Mel was a computer programmer from Pease Pottage, with a photographic memory. She had a passion for exercise and healthy living, which she tried to pass on to the Sixth Doctor, prescribing carrot juice and an exercise bike regime. The Doctor first encountered her during his trial by the Time Lords, though she already knew him, having travelled with him in his own future. Friendly, honest and rather gullible, Mel tended to trust everyone she met, a quality that often put her in danger. She travelled with the Seventh Doctor until she decided to stay with and attempt to reform the criminal Sabalom Glitz.

Story **Time and the Rani** ⊕ Written by **Pip & Jane Baker** ⊕ Featuring **the Seventh Doctor and Mel** ⊕ Foe **the Rani, the Tetraps** ⊕ First broadcast **7–28 September 1987** ⊕ **4 episodes**

Story **Paradise Towers** ⊕ Written by **Stephen Wyatt** ⊕ Featuring **the Seventh Doctor and Mel** ⊕ Foe **Kroagnon** ⊕ First broadcast **5–26 October 1987** ⊕ **4 episodes**

Story **Delta and the Bannermen** ⊕ Written by **Malcolm Kohll** ⊕ Featuring **the Seventh Doctor and Mel** ⊕ Foe **Gavrok, the Bannermen** ⊕ First broadcast **2–16 November 1987** ⊕ **3 episodes**

ACE

Played by **Sophie Aldred** First appearance **Dragonfire (1987)**
Last appearance **Survival (1989)**

The production team considered replacing Mel with either
Delta and the Bannermen's Ray, played by
Sara Griffiths, or Dragonfire's Ace,
played by Sophie Aldred in her
first television role.
A rebellious tomboy
who lied about her age
(16 not
18),
Ace
was one
of the
'wolves
of Fenric'
– unwitting
human
carriers of
Fenric's evil.
Imprisoned by the Doctor
centuries earlier, Fenric now caused a time storm
to tear Ace from her home in 1980s Perivale and dump her
on Iceworld, where she met the Doctor. Recognising Fenric's
influence, the Doctor took her
with him in the TARDIS.

INTRUSION COUNTERMEASURES GROUP

With an unidentified extraterrestrial
threat concealed in a London
junkyard in 1963, an ad
hoc military team was
hastily assembled. Group
Captain 'Chunky' Gilmore
led a small force of
regular army troops, with
Professor Rachel Jensen
and her assistant Allison
Williams drafted in from
Cambridge under the
Peacetime Emergency
Powers Act to give
scientifc support. When the Doctor arrived, he revealed that
the alien was a Dalek, and two rival Dalek factions were soon
fighting in London's streets.

Story **Dragonfire** ☺ Written by **Ian Briggs** ☺
Featuring **the Seventh Doctor, Mel and Ace** ☺
Foe **Kane** ☺ First broadcast **23 November–7
December 1987** ☺ **3 episodes**

Story **Remembrance of the Daleks** ☺ Written
by **Ben Aaronovitch** ☺ Featuring **the Seventh
Doctor and Ace** ☺ Foe **the Daleks, Davros**
☺ First broadcast **5–26 October 1988** ☺ **4
episodes**

Story **The Happiness Patrol** ☺ Written by
Graeme Curry ☺ Featuring **the Seventh Doctor
and Ace** ☺ Foe **Helen A, the Kandy Man** ☺ First
broadcast ☺ 1? November 1988 ☺ 3 episodes

Story **Silver Nemesis** ☻ Written by **Kevin Clarke** ☻ Featuring **the Seventh Doctor and Ace** ☻ Foe the **Cybermen, Lady Peinforte** ☻ First broadcast **23 November–7 December 1988** ☻ **3 episodes**

Story **The Greatest Show in the Galaxy** ☻ Written by **Stephen Wyatt** ☻ Featuring **the Seventh Doctor and Ace** ☻ Foe **the Gods of Ragnarok** ☻ First broadcast **14 December 1988–4 January 1989** ☻ **4 episodes**

Story **Battlefield** ☻ Written by **Ben Aaronovitch** ☻ Featuring **the Seventh Doctor, Ace and UNIT** ☻ Foe **Morgaine, the Destroyer** ☻ First broadcast **6–27 September 1989** ☻ **4 episodes**

Insecure, volatile and easily bored, Ace claimed to loathe her mother, not least because she had given her the name Dorothy. She wore a jacket covered in badges, revealing her desire to belong despite her overt rejection of being part of any society or group. Her only real enthusiasm at school had been for chemistry, until she was suspended for blowing up the art room and started work in a fast-food café. She specialised in devising home-made bombs – the Doctor was forever cautioning her against using Nitro-9, an unstable explosive she carried in old deodorant cans.

Ace did, though, share many of the Doctor's ideals, her instinctive anti-racism, impulsive hatred of oppression and dislike of hypocrisy and betrayal matching his own, and she

THE BRIGADIER

Returning once more to *Doctor Who* in 1989, Nicholas Courtney agreed that the Brigadier should finally go out in a blaze of glory. The production team ultimately thought better of plans to kill off the character, and the Brigadier lived to fight another day.

Called out of retirement in the 1990s by the UN Secretary-General, Lethbridge-Stewart was sent to Carbury, where a UNIT convoy was stranded in the middle of a battle between knights from another dimension. The Brigadier delighted in demonstrating to the Doctor how well-equipped modern UNIT was, and used silver bullets to kill an entity called the Destroyer.

quickly developed a profound faith in the Doctor. He saw her as a student of sorts, and their adventures were sometimes contrived to enable her to confront her insecurities: he once took her to a Victorian mansion, which a younger Ace would burn down a century later. A visit to a naval base in 1943 brought Ace face to face with her mother Audrey as a baby. With Haemovores attacking the base, Ace sent the infant Audrey to her nan's house in London, inadvertently creating her own future.

Story **Ghost Light** ☺ Written by **Marc Platt** ☺ Featuring **the Seventh Doctor and Ace** ☺ Foe **Light, Josiah Smith** ☺ First broadcast **4–18 October 1989** ☺ **3 episodes**

Story **The Curse of Fenric** ☺ Written by **Ian Briggs** ☺ Featuring **the Seventh Doctor and Ace** ☺ Foe **Fenric, the Haemovores** ☺ First broadcast **25 October–15 November 1989** ☺ **4 episodes**

Story **Survival** ☺ Written by **Rona Munro** ☺ Featuring **the Seventh Doctor and Ace** ☺ Foe the **Master, the Cheetah People** ☺ First broadcast 11 ▯▯▯▯▯▯▯▯▯▯▯▯▯▯▯▯▯▯▯▯▯▯▯▯▯▯

GRACE HOLLOWAY

Played by **Daphne Ashbrook** Guest appearance **Doctor Who (1996)**

Six years after the end of Season 26, Doctor Who returned with a one-off television movie, in which Sylvester McCoy's Seventh Doctor regenerated into Paul McGann's Eighth, facing the end of the world at the turn of the millennium. The film was a co-production by the BBC and America's Fox Network and Universal Studios, and was filmed in Canada with a mostly American cast and crew. The 'companion' figure for the story – although she didn't go on to travel with the Doctor – was played by Daphne Ashbrook, who had appeared in more than 30 different TV series over the previous 12 years, including Star Trek: Deep Space Nine, Murder She Wrote and Falcon Crest.

Travelling alone and diverted by the Master to San Francisco on 31 December 1999, the Doctor was caught in a gangland war and shot down. Although the bullets did little actual damage, the Doctor's hearts were beating dangerously fast, so hospital staff – dismissing his twin hearts as a double-exposed X-ray – called in cardiologist Grace Holloway. Dr Holloway was unable to cope with her patient's alien biology, and the Doctor died.

Grace Holloway was Walker General Hospital's senior cardiologist. Intelligent and principled, she became a doctor because she had always dreamed of holding back death. She was appalled when the hospital

administrator, Swift, covered up her patient's demise rather than risk adverse publicity, and she resigned when Swift burnt the X-ray evidence of the Doctor's alien make-up. She showed the same independence when faced with a stranger claiming to be her deceased patient, arguing against the impossibility of his claims but open-minded enough to consider the available evidence of his double heartbeat and non-human blood. She veered between scepticism and awestruck delight as she heard wild claims about a rival alien genius threatening the destruction of the world as a side effect of his quest to steal the Doctor's remaining lives. But, confronted by the TARDIS interior and witnessing the Master's actions, she had to accept the Doctor's story.

Story **Doctor Who** ❀ Written by **Mathew Jacobs** ❀ Featuring **the Seventh and Eighth Doctors, Grace and Chang Lee** ❀ Foe **the Master** ❀ First UK broadcast **27 May 1996** ❀ **1 episode**

Grace's ability to think on her feet saved not just the planet but also her own life. When the Master killed her, she had already set the TARDIS in a temporal orbit. Briefly existing outside space and time, the time machine itself resurrected her.

Grace was a music lover, and listened to Puccini's *Madam Butterfly* while she operated on the Doctor – something that drew him to her after his regeneration. Though attracted to the Doctor she turned down his invitation to join him in the TARDIS, suggesting that he stay with her instead.

CHANG LEE

Caught up in San Francisco's gang culture, Chang Lee got the Doctor to hospital after he had been shot. But when he was told of the Doctor's death on the operating table, Chang Lee stole the Doctor's possessions and made a quick getaway. Intrigued by the assortment of strange objects – jelly babies, sonic screwdriver, TARDIS key – he made his way back to the TARDIS, where he encountered the Master. Discovering that the TARDIS systems responded to the boy, the Master convinced Chang Lee to help him, promising wealth and power.

Lee eventually stood up to him when he realised the Master had been lying. Like Grace, Chang Lee was killed by the Master but was revived during the TARDIS's temporal orbit. With the world saved and the Master defeated, the Doctor gave Chang Lee a bag of gold and advised him to get out of San Francisco.

ROSE TYLER

Played by **Billie Piper** First appearance **Rose (2005)**
Last regular appearance **Doomsday (2006)** Guest appearances **Partners in Crime, Turn Left, The Stolen Earth** and **Journey's End (2008)**

With Doctor Who recommissioned by the BBC after a second long absence, head writer Russell T Davies set about placing the 'companion' figure at the heart of the series. The programme's template had always included human characters for audience members to identify with. Rose Tyler, however, was going to be much more than that: she would be our eyes and ears. We would see the wonders of time and space from her point of view. And Rose would be in many ways the Doctor's equal, reflected in the shared billing in the opening titles of each episode and in the casting, alongside Christopher Eccleston, of Billie Piper. Her acting career had been interrupted when

she became a major pop star at 15, one of the youngest chart-toppers the UK had ever known, but by 2004 she was already establishing herself as a significant presence on film and television. Notable appearances included lead roles in Bella and the Boys **and** The Canterbury Tales. When Doctor Who was officially relaunched in March 2005, a series of trailers included Rose asking which the viewer would choose – an ordinary life on Earth or time travel with the Doctor. Almost 11 million chose the TARDIS, and Rose Tyler became both an instant mainstream hit and a hero to a whole new child audience, especially girls, who helped to firmly establish the revived series as one of Britain's biggest dramas.

Nineteen years old, living with her mum on a South London council estate and working in Henrik's department store, Rose Tyler was bored with her mundane life. When the Doctor offered her the trip of a lifetime, nothing would ever be the same again.

The Doctor had been travelling alone since the end of the Time War, and he had no real wish for a new companion. But Rose quickly impressed him with her quick-thinking resourcefulness and proved herself in many ways the Doctor's equal. She saved him from the Nestene Consciousness and argued against executing the last Dalek,

Story **Rose** ☺ Written by **Russell T Davies** ☺ Featuring **the Ninth Doctor and Rose with Jackie and Mickey** ☺ For the Nestene Consciousness, the Autons ☺ First broadcast **26 March 2005** ☺ 1 episode

pointing out that the Doctor was changing into something he hated. Rose often challenged the Doctor's decisions and sometimes his morality – she would not condone using Gwyneth and was reluctant to accept the idea of the Gelth inhabiting and reanimating corpses to survive. At first daunted by a host of alien species aboard Platform One, she quickly adapted and began to understand the Doctor's description of them as 'people'.

Fond as she was of her mum Jackie and boyfriend Mickey, Rose barely hesitated when given the chance to travel and didn't think through the possible effects on them. She was horrified to discover her 12-month absence had left Jackie distraught and Mickey under police suspicion, but still couldn't resist continuing her travels with the Doctor.

Story **The End of the World** ☻ Written by **Russell T Davies** ☻ Featuring **the Ninth Doctor and Rose** with **Jackie** ☻ Foe **Cassandra** ☻ First broadcast **2 April 2005** ☻ **1 episode**

Story **The Unquiet Dead** ☻ Written by **Mark Gatiss** ☻ Featuring **the Ninth Doctor and Rose** ☻ Foe **the Gelth** ☻ First broadcast **9 April 2005** ☻ **1 episode**

JABE

Jabe of the Forest of Cheem was on Platform One for the Earthdeath event. Having established a rapport with the Doctor, sympathising with his loss of his people, she gave her life helping him reach the manual reset switch for Platform One's defences.

GWYNETH

The maidservant Gwyneth had psychic powers caused by living near Cardiff's Rift. She voluntarily acted as a gateway for the Gelth to enter this universe. This killed her, but she managed to destroy the Gelth by igniting the gas in Sneed's morgue.

JACKIE TYLER

Played by **Camille Coduri** First appearance **Rose (2005)** Last regular appearance
Doomsday (2006) Guest appearance **Journey's End (2008)**

Russell T Davies wanted to give Rose Tyler a detailed and believable background,
and he created a family for her to which the TARDIS could regularly return as
an anchor for the series' explorations of time and
space. Cast as Rose's mum was Camille Coduri,
who had starred in Rumpole of the Bailey,
The History of Tom Jones and many other
series and films since 1987.

Jackie Tyler was a
single mum, working out
of her council flat as a
hairdresser. Naturally
chatty and friendly,
she began flirting with the Doctor
as soon as she laid eyes on him.
When they next met, she slapped
him, furious at Rose's year-long
disappearance. Having spent
that year searching for her
missing daughter, Jackie
was disappointed when
Rose left again. But her
resentment towards the
Doctor softened when he
fulfilled his promise to keep Rose
safe, sending her home from the Game
Station against her wishes.

Story **Aliens of London** and **World War Three** ❂ Written
by **Russell T Davies** ❂ Featuring **the Ninth Doctor and
Rose with Jackie, Mickey and UNIT** ❂ Foe **the Slitheen**
❂ First broadcast **16–23 April 2005** ❂ **2 episodes**

Story **Dalek** ❂ Written by **Robert Shearman** ❂ Featuring
the Ninth Doctor and Rose with Adam ❂ Foe **Dalek** ❂
First broadcast **30 April 2005** ❂ **1 episode**

PETE TYLER

Peter Alan Tyler died in a car accident in November 1987 when Rose was still a baby. Taken to the scene by the Doctor, 19-year-old Rose couldn't resist saving her father, creating a wound in time through which came deadly Reapers that threatened to wipe out humanity. Pete worked out that the strange girl who'd saved him was his daughter, accepting her explanation that she had travelled in time. When the Reapers consumed the Doctor, Pete sacrificed himself, running out in front of the car that should have killed him and so saving the world.

ADAM MITCHELL

A self-proclaimed genius, Adam worked for Henry Van Statten in Utah in 2012, cataloguing alien artefacts. The Doctor took him to an orbiting satellite in 200,000, but Adam saw time travel as a means of helping himself, attempting to gain information from the future and send it back to the 21st century – furious, the Doctor took Adam home.

After that, Jackie had a better relationship with the Doctor, while her dislike of Rose's ex-boyfriend also lessened, as she and Mickey were united in missing Rose.

Having lost her husband 19 years earlier, Jackie's flirtatious nature helped counter her loneliness. She went out with a series of men, though she never forgot Pete Tyler and used to show Rose old family photographs and tell stories of him.

Jackie's life was to change for ever when her first trip in the TARDIS took her to the Torchwood Institute, where she was caught up in events involving Cybermen, Daleks and a group of people from a parallel version of Earth…

Story **The Long Game** ☻ Written by **Russell T Davies** ☻ Featuring **the Ninth Doctor and Rose with Adam** ☻ Foe **the Jagrafess** ☻ First broadcast 7 May 2005 ☻ 1 episode

Story **Father's Day** ☻ Written by **Paul Cornell** ☻ Featuring **the Ninth Doctor and Rose with Jackie** ☻ Foe **the Reapers** ☻ First broadcast 14 May 2005 ☻ 1 episode

CAPTAIN JACK

Played by **John Barrowman** First appearance **The Empty Child (2005)** Last regular
appearance **The Parting of the Ways (2005)** Guest appearances **Utopia, The Sound of
Drums** and **Last of the Time Lords (2007), The Stolen Earth** and **Journey's End (2008)**

Actor, dancer, singer, presenter and author John Barrowman is a lifelong Doctor Who fan, who
has claimed he screamed with joy in the middle of London's Covent Garden when told that he
had won a semi-regular part in the
series. Born in Scotland but raised
in the USA, he initially played Jack for five
episodes before the character was given his
own spin-off series, Torchwood.

Captain Jack Harkness,
real name unknown, was
an ex-time agent from
the 51st century,
who grew up on
the Boeshane
Peninsula where
he was nicknamed the Face of Boe. Discovering that the
Time Agency had erased two years from his memory, he
quit and became a conman, meeting Rose and the Doctor
when he tried to trick them into buying a 'harmless piece
of space junk'. The Doctor was wary of him at first, but
quickly grew to rely on his ingenuity and technical know-
how. Though he presented a carefully crafted persona — funny,
funny, sexy and arrogant — Jack was a brave and experienced

Story **The Empty Child** and **The
Doctor Dances** ☺ Written by
Steven Moffat ☺ Featuring **the
Ninth Doctor, Rose and Captain
Jack** ☺ Foe **Nanogenes** ☺ First
broadcast **21–28 May 2005** ☺ **2
episodes**

soldier, and he led the defence of the Game Station when it was attacked by the Daleks in 200,100. Jack knew he would die to buy the Doctor time to defeat the Daleks, and he was the last man standing as they reached their goal. When Rose, filled with the power of the Vortex, brought him back to life, she inadvertently left him unable to die. Sensing this, the Doctor abandoned him, and Jack had to use his Vortex Manipulator to escape to 19th-century Cardiff. Proving his loyalty to the Doctor, Jack waited on Earth for 139 years, joining Torchwood and then, after its destruction in the Battle of Canary Wharf, remodelling it as a tribute to the Doctor.

LYNDA MOSS & THE GAME STATION CONTROLLER

Wired into the Game Station systems by the Daleks when she was 5 years old, the Controller betrayed her masters' location to the Doctor, knowing it would cost her her life. She was the first of many to die in the battle against the Daleks. Captain Jack organised a small band of defenders, among them Lynda Moss, who had met the Doctor as a Big Brother contestant and hoped to travel with him. She died monitoring the Daleks' progress through the Station.

Story **Boom Town** ☻ Written by **Russell T Davies** ☻ Featuring **the Ninth Doctor, Rose and Captain Jack** with Mickey ☻ Foe **the Slitheen** ☻ First broadcast **4 June 2005** ☻ 1 episode

Story **Bad Wolf** and **The Parting of the
Ways** ☻ Written by **Russell T Davies** ☻
Featuring **the Ninth Doctor, Rose and
Captain Jack with Jackie, Mickey and
the Tenth Doctor** ☻ Foe **the Daleks,
the Emperor Dalek** ☻ First broadcast
11–18 June 2005 ☻ **2 episodes**

Bad Wolf

Faced with almost half a million Daleks, the Doctor
was determined to keep Rose safe and tricked her
into returning home. As she explained to Jackie and
Mickey how important the Doctor was – not just to
her, but to all of them – she decided that she could
not abandon him to fight
on everyone's behalf. She
realised that the phrase 'Bad
Wolf', which they'd come
across everywhere they
went, was not a threat but
a message, telling her that
she could still get back to
the Doctor. Forcing open
the TARDIS console, she
absorbed the power of
the Vortex. She became
the Bad Wolf, gaining
godlike abilities with

which she destroyed the Dalek fleet, saving the
Doctor and resurrecting Captain Jack.

But Rose could not control the Vortex energy,
which threatened to destroy her, and the Doctor
drew it from her and into himself, precipitating
his own death and regeneration. The Doctor
tried to warn her that he was about to change,
but Rose was unprepared for the sight of a
complete stranger inside the TARDIS.

Harriet Jones

Harriet Jones, the self-effacing backbench MP for Flydale North, was in 10 Downing Street to discuss cottage hospitals when she found herself trapped with the Doctor, Rose and a group of Slitheen. With the Prime Minister murdered and 10 Downing Street in ruins, it was Harriet who emerged at the end of the crisis to reassure the world that the threat had passed. By the end of the year, she had been elected Prime Minister with a landslide majority at the start of what should have been a Golden Age. But her decision to order an invading Sycorax ship shot down enraged the Doctor, who brought down her government. Convinced that she had done the right thing, Harriet devoted herself to protecting Earth. When she used a Subwave Network to establish contact with the Doctor during the Dalek attack, the invaders exterminated her.

YOU!

With Rose in 1979 watching ABBA and a Graske wrecking people's Christmases, the Doctor enlisted an unknown human. Guided remotely by the Doctor, this young person helped pilot the TARDIS and tracked the Graske from Earth to its home planet of Griffoth. The Doctor guided his new friend through a series of logic traps leading to the Graske control centre, where he or she transmatted the creature's captives back to their homes and time zones. This young human has never been identified. Was it you?

Story **Born Again** ⊛ Written by **Russell T Davies** ⊛ Featuring **the Tenth Doctor and Rose** ⊛ First broadcast **18 November 2005** ⊛ **1 episode**

Story **The Christmas Invasion** ⊛ Written by **Russell T Davies** ⊛ Featuring **the Tenth Doctor and Rose with Jackie, Mickey and UNIT** ⊛ Foe **Roboforms, the Sycorax** ⊛ First broadcast **25 December 2005** ⊛ **1 episode**

Story **Attack of the Graske** ⊛ Written by **Gareth Roberts** ⊛ Featuring **the Tenth Doctor** ⊛ Foe **the Graske** ⊛ First broadcast **25 December 2005** ⊛ **1 episode**

Story **New Earth** ⊛ Written by **Russell T Davies** ⊛ Featuring **the Tenth Doctor and Rose with Jackie and Mickey** ⊛ Foe **Cassandra** ⊛ First broadcast **15 April 2006** ⊛ **1 episode**

Just the latest in a long line?

Rose was quickly convinced of the new Doctor's authenticity when he took on the Sycorax, and she resumed her travels with him. Though she had been devastated to lose 'her' Doctor, she soon found that she had an even closer relationship with his successor, and they revelled in their adventures, scoffing at the idea of returning to the TARDIS rather than facing danger on Krop Tor, and marvelling at encountering both a werewolf and Queen Victoria – though the latter was distinctly unamused by their attitude and founded Torchwood to defend Earth, with the Doctor listed as its number one enemy.

Much as she was enjoying herself, Rose found that she might not be as special to the Doctor as she hoped. She was bewildered when the Doctor casually mentioned he had once been a father, and livid when he let Mickey join them in the TARDIS. The Doctor's willingness to sacrifice himself to save Madame de Pompadour from the clockwork robots also affected her, and she tried to play up her closeness to him at Mickey's expense, excluding him from their remiscences of earlier adventures. Perhaps the greatest shock, though, was the discovery that the Doctor had had other travelling companions before her, forcing her to consider that she might not be with him for ever.

You were my life

After the Doctor left her in Aberdeen, abruptly ending their travels, Sarah Jane Smith struggled to adjust to life back on Earth. She felt abandoned by the man who, she realised, had been her life, though she never lost her bravery, sense of justice or nose for a news story.

Reports of strange lights in the sky and abnormal school results brought her to Deffry Vale High School, where she met the Doctor for the first time in a quarter of a century. The fight against the Krillitanes and the chance to talk things through with the Doctor helped make Sarah Jane more willing to make the most of her life away from the TARDIS and, by the time the Doctor next saw her, she had an adopted son and, alongside his schoolfriends, K-9 and a supercomputer, was once again helping defend Earth from hostile aliens. When the Earth was transported to the Medusa Cascade and the Daleks attacked, Sarah Jane surrendered so she could get to the Dalek command ship. She was armed with a Warp Star and was prepared to use it to destroy the Daleks if all else failed.

REINETTE, MADAME DE POMPADOUR

One of the most accomplished women of the 18th century, Reinette Poisson made an instant impression on the Doctor when he discovered 51st-century clockwork robots tracking her through her timeline. Her many talents unexpectedly included the ability to read the Doctor's mind as he read hers, and she was astute enough to grasp the fantastic concepts – spaceships, time travel, robots – she encountered.

MICKEY SMITH

Played by **Noel Clarke** First appearance **Rose (2005)** Last regular appearance **Doomsday (2006)** Guest appearance **Journey's End (2008)**

Another key element of Russell T Davies's plans to give Rose a believable family background was her on/off boyfriend Mickey. After a week of auditions, Noel Clarke was cast, though his commitments on Auf Wiedersehen, Pet clashed with Doctor Who's own recording schedules, so filming dates for Rose and Aliens of London had to be adjusted.

Mickey Smith was Rose Tyler's boyfriend when she first met the Doctor during the Nestene invasion. Swallowed by a Nestene-controlled wheelie bin, held captive in the alien's lair and duplicated, Mickey's usually laid-back attitude crumbled – terrified, he was automatically suspicious of the alien Doctor who

PARALLEL PETE

On parallel Earth, Pete Tyler had survived to become a successful businessman – with no daughter, though still married to Jackie. This Pete recognised the dangers in the creation of the Cybormon and leaked information to try to stop it. He was too late, and his wife was among thousands converted to Cyberform. But when the Cybermen crossed from his world to ours and battled Daleks at the Torchwood Institute, Pete found himself with a new family, as Rose, Jackie and Mickey were trapped in the parallel world.

Story **Tooth and Claw** Written by **Russell T Davies** Featuring **the Tenth Doctor and Rose** Foe **werewolf** First broadcast **22 April 2006** **1 episode**

Story **School Reunion** Written by **Toby Whithouse** Featuring **the Tenth Doctor and Rose with Mickey, Sarah Jane, K-9 Mk III and K-9 Mk IV** Foe **the Krillitanes** First broadcast **29 April 2006** **1 episode**

Story **The Girl in the Fireplace** Written by **Steven Moffat** Featuring **the Tenth Doctor, Rose and Mickey** Foe **clockwork robots** First broadcast **6 May 2006** **1 episode**

Story **Rise of the Cybermen** and **The Age of Steel** Written by **Tom MacRae** Featuring **the Tenth Doctor, Rose and Mickey with Jackie** Foe **the Cybermen** First broadcast **13–20 May 2006** **2 episodes**

Rose had hooked up with. For Mickey, being abandoned by his girlfriend was made worse when Rose's disappearance led to 12 months of suspicion from Jackie, his neighbours and the police, but he stayed loyal to her. When the Doctor and Rose returned, Mickey's computer skills played a vital part in defeating the Slitheen and the Doctor, who had constantly teased him by getting his name wrong and calling him an idiot, recognised this and offered him a place in the TARDIS. Mickey refused, though he later thought better of it and joined them after all. This led him to a parallel Earth, where he saw his own double killed by Cybermen. Finding his gran was alive on parallel Earth, fed up of being regarded as 'the tin dog', and realising that Rose would never leave the Doctor for him, Mickey elected to stay there, joining a fight against the Cybermen which would eventually lead him back to our universe.

Story **The Idiot's Lantern** ☻ Written by **Mark Gatiss** ☻ Featuring **the Tenth Doctor and Rose** ☻ Foe **the Wire** ☻ First broadcast **27 May 2006** ☻ **1 episode**

Story **The Impossible Planet** and **The Satan Pit** ☻ Written by **Matt Jones** ☻ Featuring **the Tenth Doctor and Rose** ☻ Foe **the Beast, the Ood** ☻ First broadcast **3–10 June 2006** ☻ **2 episodes**

Story **Love & Monsters** ☻ Written by **Russell T Davies** ☻ Featuring **the Tenth Doctor and Rose with Jackie** ☻ Foe **the Abzorbaloff** ☻ First broadcast **17 June 2006** ☻ **1 episode**

They keep trying to split us up

Alone together after Mickey's departure, the Doctor and Rose travelled on, exploring new worlds, defeating alien menaces and having fun. Equally fearless and resourceful, they frequently found themselves separated – Rose lost her face and life force to the Wire, the Doctor vanished into an Isolus's fantasy world, and Rose found herself fleeing a black hole in a rocket while the Doctor was trapped in a pit far below the impossible planet's surface. As the Doctor told the Beast, though, if he had faith in anything it was in Rose – the Doctor sent the Beast's body into the black hole while Rose dealt with the possessed human who carried the Beast's mind. And, just as the Doctor's drive to stop the Wire was fuelled by losing

L.I.N.D.A.

Colin Skinner, Bridget, Ursula Blake, Elton Pope and Bliss had all noticed that the Doctor had been around during each of the strange events and alien attacks of recent years. But their weekly meetings slowly lost focus on the Doctor, as cookery, novel-writing and music took over, until Victor Kennedy arrived. Actually a disguised alien from the planet Clom, he set them to work hunting for the Doctor and Rose. Bliss, Bridget, Colin and Ursula were all absorbed by the creature, which Elton named the Abzorbaloff, but they fought back when he tried to force the Doctor to hand over the TARDIS. When Elton destroyed the Abzorbaloff's limitation field, the creature burst and was absorbed into the pavement.

Story **Fear Her** ⊛ Written by **Matthew Graham** ⊛ Featuring **the Tenth Doctor and Rose** ⊛ First broadcast **24 June 2006** ⊛ **1 episode**

Story **Army of Ghosts** and **Doomsday** ⊛ Written by **Russell T Davies** ⊛ Featuring **the Tenth Doctor and Rose with Jackie and Mickey** ⊛ Foe **the Cybermen, the Daleks** ⊛ First broadcast **1–8 July 2006** ⊛ **2 episodes**

Rose, so she was determined to solve the Isolus problem and rescue him.

When millions of parallel Earth Cybermen and four Daleks attacked our world, Mickey followed them through the Void and, impossibly, Rose's parents were 'reunited'. The only solution to the Dalek and Cybermen invasions was to send them back into the Void, but the Doctor realised that Rose, too, would be sucked through the breach. To keep her safe, he sent her to parallel Earth with her family, but Rose decided the Doctor was more important to her and returned, accepting that she would never see Jackie again. The Daleks and Cybermen were sent into the Void, with Rose almost joining them. Saved by Pete, she became trapped on parallel Earth.

In what they thought was their final conversation, Rose realised that she was in love with the Doctor. She did not hear his reply, as the breach between the two realities sealed, separating them seemingly for ever. While Jackie and Pete began a new family – having a son called Tony – and Mickey moved his gran into Pete's mansion, Rose still hoped to be reunited with the Doctor. Working for Torchwood, she was involved in the development of a Dimension Cannon which would eventually enable her to cross back to her universe…

DONNA NOBLE

Played by **Catherine Tate**
Guest appearance **The Runaway Bride (2006)** First regular appearance
Partners in Crime (2008) Last appearance **Journey's End (2008)**

When Billie Piper left, Russell T Davies already had plans for her replacement in
Series Three, but he also wanted an instant, headline-grabbing event to end Series
Two and lead into The Runaway Bride. Contracted for the surprise cameo and
subsequent co-starring role in the 2006 Christmas special, comedian and actor
Catherine Tate enjoyed working on Doctor Who so much that she leapt at the
chance to return a year later as a regular companion.

Donna Noble, an office temp from Chiswick, had
an unwelcome introduction to the Doctor when
she suddenly appeared inside the TARDIS on
her wedding day. A victim of the Empress of the
Racnoss's plans to revive her hibernating offspring,
Donna had been dosed with Huon particles by her
fiancé Lance, who, she discovered, had never
really loved her and was only with her on the
Empress's orders. Lance was contemptuous
of Donna's ignorance of the wider world
and her obsession with trivia, celebrity and
gossip. As the Doctor quickly realised, though,
Lance was wrong to assume Donna was
unintelligent – quick-thinking, courageous and
brash, Donna refused to be kept out of danger
and, crucially, was there to stop the Doctor going
too far in defeating the Empress. Having witnessed
the creation of the Earth and the destruction of the
Racnoss, she quickly recognised how much more there was
to the universe, but she baulked at joining the Doctor in the
TARDIS – a decision Donna would soon regret.

Story **The Runaway Bride** ⊕
Written by **Russell T Davies**
⊕ Featuring **the Tenth Doctor
and Donna with Sylvia** ⊕ Foe
**Performed, the Empress of
the Racnoss** ⊕ First broadcast
25 December 2006 ⊕ 1
episode

MARTHA JONES

Played by **Freema Agyeman** First appearance **Smith and Jones (2007)** Last regular appearance **Last of the Time Lords (2007)** Guest appearances **The Sontaran Stratagem, The Poison Sky, The Doctor's Daughter, The Stolen Earth** and **Journey's End (2008)**

Having cast two very well-known actors as Rose and Donna, the production team decided the new companion should be a relative 'unknown'. Freema Agyeman had appeared in several high-profile TV series, including The Bill, Casualty and the briefly revived Crossroads, but Martha Jones was her first starring role. She soon became an enthusiastic ambassador for Doctor Who, with regular appearances on Totally Doctor Who, Blue Peter and more, and made a successful crossover to spin-off series Torchwood before returning for several episodes of Series Four.

Martha Jones was a medical student at the Royal Hope, soon to qualify as a doctor, when the hospital was stolen by the Judoon. Astonished as she was to find herself on the moon watching real aliens marching across its surface in pursuit of a fugitive Plasmavore, Martha remained calm, immediately starting to think through what had happened and how the patients and staff were still alive and able to breathe. Impressed by Martha's level-headed intelligence, the Doctor happily let her join his investigation, though she took some convincing that he, too, was an alien. Ultimately, he owed his life to her – when the Plasmavore drank his blood, Martha gave her last breath to resuscitate him – and it was Martha who deduced that the Doctor's alien blood would not hide the Plasmavore from the Judoon. Impressed as he was with Martha, the Doctor was reluctant to take on a new companion so soon after being parted from Rose. He offered her a trip in the TARDIS, but constantly emphasised that she was not a replacement for Rose. In fact, the Doctor failed to notice Martha's feelings for him and frequently and inadvertently upset her by seeming to compare her with Rose. He could not, though, overlook her reliability and sheer guts in the face of Carrionites, car-jackers and Daleks and, when she confronted him over his unwillingness to open up to her, told her about the Time War and the loss of his people. By the time they had dealt with the mutated Professor Lazarus, with Martha again risking her life to lure the creature into a trap, the Doctor had accepted Martha as more than just a passenger.

Story **Smith and Jones** ☺ Written by **Russell T Davies** ☺ Featuring **the Tenth Doctor and Martha** with **Francine, Tish, Leo and Clive** ☺ Foe **the Judoon, Plasmavore, Slabs** ☺ First broadcast **31 March 2007** ☺ **1 episode**

Story **The Shakespeare Code** ☺ Written by **Gareth Roberts** ☺ Featuring **the Tenth Doctor and Martha** ☺ Foe **the Carrionites** ☺ First broadcast **7 April 2007** ☺ **1 episode**

Story **Gridlock** ☺ Written by **Russell T Davies** ☺ Featuring **the Tenth Doctor and Martha** ☺ Foe **the Macra** ☺ First broadcast **14 April 2007** ☺ **1 episode**

Story **Daleks in Manhattan and Evolution of the Daleks** ☺ Written by **Helen Raynor** ☺ Featuring **the Tenth Doctor and Martha** ☺ Foe **the Daleks** ☺ First broadcast **21–28 April 2007** ☺ **2 episodes**

THE FACE OF BOE

The Face of Boe was a huge head housed in a mobile tank, whose incredible longevity spanned some five billion years. Many legends surrounded him, including one that he had a last great secret for a lonely traveller. His final meeting with the Doctor was in New New York, when he gave the last of his power to save the city. Before he died, he revealed his secret to the Doctor, telling him: 'You Are Not Alone'.

FRANCINE AND TISH JONES

Francine played by **Adjoa Andoh** First appearance **Smith and Jones (2007)** Last regular appearance **Last of the Time Lords (2007)** Guest appearance **Journey's End (2008)** Tish played by **Gugu Mbatha-Raw** First appearance **Smith and Jones (2007)** Last appearance **Last of the Time Lords (2007)**

Like Rose, the new companion was given a family to help ground the series. Adjoa Andoh's extensive acting career had already included an appearance under layers of Catkind prosthetics as Sister Jatt in New Earth, while Gugu Mbatha-Raw had been seen in Spooks and Bad Girls. Tish was a PR officer who relied on her younger sister Martha to deal with the fallout from their parents' separation and resented their father's new girlfriend. She accepted Martha's new friend, realising her sister was happy, while their mother, Francine, was hugely suspicious of him. The Doctor received a slap from her after a Saxon employee fed her disinformation about him, and ended up unwittingly helping the Master lure Martha and the Doctor into a trap. Both Francine and Tish suffered through and remembered 'the year that never was' of the Master's reign.

CLIVE AND LEO JONES

Leo had left home to live with his girlfriend and their new baby shortly before his 21st birthday, which left Francine, a successful businesswoman, alone in the family home, since her husband Clive had left her for a younger woman called Annalise. Suffering a mid-life crisis, Clive added a flashy sports car to the mix, but proved to share some of Tish and Martha's resolve when he refused to cooperate with Saxon in entrapping Martha. Clive, Francine

and Tish were all enslaved aboard the *Valiant*, where they joined an attempted

revolt against the Master. There were even signs that Clive and Francine might be reconciled after their trauma. Leo, meanwhile, proved that he was smarter than he looked when the Master interrupted a call between him and Martha. He heeded Martha's warning and went into hiding. He was therefore the only member of the Jones family not to remember the year's events after time was reversed.

Frequent flyer

Martha, now acknowledged by the Doctor as a fully fledged travelling companion complete with 'superphone' and TARDIS key, was devoted to the Doctor and willing to risk everything for him. She still sometimes found it hard to accept that he would not return her feelings for him and, though she found herself attracted to *Pentallian* crewmember Riley, she didn't consider staying with him. On the wreck of the *Infinite* soon afterwards, she was shown her 'heart's desire' – the Doctor.

But when they were hunted by the Family of Blood, a parasitic species with a very limited life span who wanted the Doctor's Time Lord

essence, he physically changed himself, taking human form and placing himself entirely in Martha's protection. As history teacher John Smith, he fell in love with a school nurse, with Martha forced to admit that her own feelings would never be reciprocated.

Though a chance encounter with Jack Harkness later brought up the subject of Rose again, Martha began to see past her feelings, and she never wavered as the Doctor's most loyal friend.

Story **The Lazarus Experiment** ❋ Written by **Stephen Greenhorn** ❋ Featuring **the Tenth Doctor and Martha with Francine, Tish and Leo** ❋ Foe **Lazarus** ❋ First broadcast **5 May 2007** ❋ **1 episode**

Story **42** ❋ Written by **Chris Chibnall** ❋ Featuring **the Tenth Doctor and Martha with Francine** ❋ Foe **the sun-possessed** ❋ First broadcast **19 May 2007** ❋ **1 episode**

Story **The Infinite Quest** ❋ Written by **Alan Barnes** ❋ Featuring **the Tenth Doctor and Martha** ❋ Foe **Baltazar** ❋ First broadcast **30 June 2007** ❋ **1 episode**

Joan Redfern

The matron at Farringdon School for Boys was Nurse Joan Redfern. A widow who had lost her husband in the Boer War, Nurse Redfern was attracted to John Smith, the new history teacher, and the two skirted politely around the issue for several weeks until she plucked up the courage to mention the Village Dance to him – the stricter social rules of 1913 made even this a daring gesture.

Unfortunately, John and Joan's growing affection coincided with the arrival of the Family of Blood, and the village was soon under attack. At first she was dismissive of Martha's efforts to persuade them that John Smith was in fact a Time Lord called the Doctor, and the only one who could save them all. The weight of evidence eventually convinced her, however, and, having read his journal of dreams of his life as the Doctor, it was Joan who persuaded John that he would have to abandon his human persona to protect them all. Fully restored, the Doctor defeated the Family before returning to Joan and asking her to travel with him and Martha – he remembered his experiences as John Smith and hoped they might be able to recapture their relationship. But Joan made the devastating observation that many people had died purely because the Doctor had chosen Farringdon to hide in, and she asked him to leave.

Story **Human Nature** and **The Family of Blood** ✤ Written by **Paul Cornell** ✤ Featuring **the Tenth Doctor and Martha** ✤ Foe **the Family of Blood, scarecrows** ✤ First broadcast **26 May–2 June 2007** ✤ **2 episodes**

Sally Sparrow

When the Doctor and Martha were attacked by Weeping Angels in Wester Drumlins house and sent back to 1969, they already knew what to do, thanks to a young woman called Sally Sparrow...

Exploring Wester Drumlins in 2007, Sally discovered a message to her from the Doctor in 1969. There followed a bizarre series of events in which her friends were sent back in time while Sally pieced together the puzzle and talked to the Doctor via a DVD of his half of the conversation which he had recorded 38 years earlier, telling her what to do. She led the Weeping Angels to the TARDIS, which was activated by the Doctor's DVD and departed for 1969, leaving the Angels trapped. A year later, Sally had compiled notes on every detail of her experience and, in a chance encounter with the Doctor earlier in his own timeline, was able to forewarn him of events at Wester Drumlins a year earlier.

Story **Blink** ❂ Written by **Steven Moffat** ❂ Featuring **the Tenth Doctor and Martha** ❂ Foe **the Weeping Angels** ❂ First broadcast **9 June 2007** ❂ **1 episode**

Story **Utopia** ❂ Written by **Russell T Davies** Featuring **the Tenth Doctor, Martha and Captain Jack** ❂ Foe **the Master, the Futurekind** ❂ First broadcast **16 June 2007** ❂ **1 episode**

Walking the Earth

The Doctor had never had to rely on anyone so completely as he did Martha Jones when the Master and the Toclafane took control of the world. With her family and Captain Jack imprisoned on the *Valiant* and the Doctor physically aged to his full 900 years, the fate of the planet was in Martha's hands. Alone, she walked across the globe for a year, and became a legend. There were rumours that she had been collecting parts for a gun which could kill the Master, but Martha had actually been inspiring the survivors with stories of the Doctor, and preparing everyone she met for the countdown to the launch of the Master's war rockets. Led by Martha, the whole world thought of the Doctor in that final moment, giving him the psychic strength to rejuvenate and end the Master's reign. Realising that the Doctor would never reciprocate her feelings for him, Martha now decided to leave the TARDIS and concentrate on helping her family get over their experiences at the hands of the Master. To her delight, Martha discovered that the Doctor had recommended her to UNIT. Her medical qualifications were fast-tracked and Doctor Jones was recruited as a UNIT medical officer.

Story **The Sound of Drums** and **Last of the Time Lords** ☺ Written by **Russell T Davies** ☺ Featuring **the Tenth Doctor, Martha and Captain Jack with Francine, Tish, Leo and Clive** ☺ Foe **the Master, the Toclafane** ☺ First broadcast **23–30 June 2007** ☺ **2 episodes**

Story **Time Crash** ☺ Written by **Steven Moffat** ☺ Featuring **the Tenth and Fifth Doctors** ☺ First broadcast **16 November 2007** ☺ **1 episode**

ASTRID PETH

Played by **Kylie Minogue** Guest appearance **Voyage of the Damned (2007)**

Hoping to top the public interest in the previous Christmas specials, Doctor Who's producers asked Kylie Minogue to play a one-off companion in Voyage of the Damned. As a former soap star and internationally successful pop star, Kylie attracted even more press coverage to the series, helping make the special one of Doctor Who's most-watched episodes ever.

Astrid Peth had always dreamed of seeing other planets and stars. As a waitress on the *Titanic*'s Christmas cruise from Sto to Earth, she was not allowed off the ship and had resigned herself to spending the voyage waiting on tables when she met the Doctor. He took her on shore leave to London, where she marvelled at the strange sights of this new and alien world. When disaster struck the *Titanic*, Astrid was among the survivors helping the Doctor make his way through the ship and the Doctor agreed to take her with him when he left. But her bravery, loyalty and compassion meant that she could not leave him to face Max Capricorn alone – with the Doctor captured by the Heavenly Host and unable to prevent Capricorn crashing the ship, Astrid sacrificed herself, using a forklift truck to push Max into the craft's engines.

Story **Voyage of the Damned**
Written by **Russell T Davies**
Featuring the **Tenth Doctor**
and a shot with **Wilf @ Foo the**
Heavenly Host, Max Capricorn
First broadcast **25 December 2007** 1 episode

Story **Partners in Crime** ⊕ Written by **Russell T Davies** ⊕ Featuring **the Tenth Doctor and Donna with Sylvia and Wilf** ⊕ Foe **Matron Cofelia, the Adipose** ⊕ First broadcast **5 April 2008** ⊕ **1 episode**

Story **The Fires of Pompeii** ⊕ Written by **James Moran** ⊕ Featuring **the Tenth Doctor and Donna** ⊕ Foe **the Pyroviles** ⊕ First broadcast **12 April 2008** ⊕ **1 episode**

Story **Planet of the Ood** ⊕ Written by **Keith Temple** ⊕ Featuring **the Tenth Doctor and Donna** ⊕ Foe **Ood Operations** ⊕ First broadcast **19 April 2008** ⊕ **1 episode**

Story **The Sontaran Stratagem** and **The Poison Sky** ⊕ Written by **Helen Raynor** ⊕ Featuring **the Tenth Doctor, Donna and Martha with Sylvia, Wilf and UNIT** ⊕ Foe **the Sontarans** ⊕ First broadcast **26 April–3 May 2008** ⊕ **2 episodes**

⊛ A Noble return

Saying goodbye to the Doctor on Christmas Day, Donna had vowed to travel the world and make something of her life. But she found that a package tour of Egypt was a poor substitute for adventures with the Doctor and resolved to track him down and take up his offer of going with him in the TARDIS. She moved back in with her mum and grandad, and spent her time following up anything unusual she read about online or in the papers. She looked into UFO sightings, crop circles, sea monsters and disappearing bees. Eventually, her investigations into Adipose Industries coincided with the Doctor's own and they were reunited. At first taken aback when she announced her intention to travel with him, the Doctor soon decided that he would enjoy having Donna alongside him, and both were relieved when she made it clear she didn't fancy him.

The Doctor had warned Donna that life in the TARDIS could be dangerous as well as exciting, which she quickly learned in Pompeii. Donna was not afraid to argue, and firmly told the Doctor that he couldn't order her around, and they disagreed over whether or not to warn the Pompeians of the impending volcanic eruption from Vesuvius. Donna was uninterested in the Doctor's description of the event as a 'fixed point' in history and wanted to try to save everybody. Yet when they discovered that the eruption was being held back by the Pyroviles and that only by causing Vesuvius to explode could the Doctor save the planet, Donna made the decision with the Doctor.

They pushed the lever together, causing the eruption that devastated Pompeii and destroyed the Pyroviles. Even then, Donna continued to argue for saving the Caecilius family, and the Doctor ultimately conceded she was right. Donna's willingness to challenge the Doctor's assumptions was a key part of their relationship – she objected to his cheap shot about slaves having made her clothes, and was first to question whether the Doctor's influence had turned Martha into a soldier. Another defining feature was Donna's tendency to tease and deflate him, happily ganging up against him with Martha and letting him complete a long farewell speech before confirming that she was just popping home for a visit. Not for the first time, the Doctor had a travelling companion who wanted to stay with him for ever.

UNIT

In the wake of attacks on Earth by Slitheen, Sycorax, Cybermen and Daleks, the Unified Intelligence Taskforce was now a better-equipped and better-funded organisation than its earlier version. UNIT moved quickly to deal with the possible threat from ATMOS and commanding officer Colonel Mace authorised Martha, now recruited to the senior ranks, to request the Doctor's help. The Doctor was typically wary of their military procedures, though Privates Harris and Jenkins were both examples of UNIT's methods being less instinctively aggressive than they once were. Faced with a Sontaran clone, Harris's response was to offer help and try to learn more about it, exactly the approach the Third Doctor had constantly urged on Brigadier Lethbridge-Stewart decades earlier.

When the Daleks attacked UNIT's New York HQ, General Sanchez ordered Martha to operate the untested Indigo Project teleport scavenged from the Sontarans and to use the Osterhagen Key. If all else failed, it was better to sacrifice the world than submit to the Daleks.

Jenny

Created in moments from a tissue sample, Jenny was the Doctor's daughter – technically, at least. She emerged from a progenation machine as a fully grown adult human but shared elements of Time Lord biology including having two hearts. Instant mental download had instilled military protocols, so she was trained and combat-ready, but she inherited the Doctor's intellectual vigour and propensity to argue, taking her father and Donna to task for thinking of her as less than human, commenting that the Doctor's strategic planning made him a sort of soldier, and noting approvingly that the 'breath of life' came from a female in Messaline's creation myth. Jenny quickly absorbed the Doctor's views on war, choosing to delay rather than shoot an opponent. But Cobb, the man she spared, later fatally shot her. The Doctor had started to accept her, and he was distraught as she died in his arms. He left with no idea that the Source's terraforming gases would soon revive her. Jenny then flew off in the colonists' ship, planning to emulate her father: saving planets, rescuing civilisations, defeating creatures and doing an awful lot of running.

River Song

When a message on his psychic paper asked him to go to The Library, the Doctor met a 51st-century archaeology professor who claimed to have known him for years. River Song was clever and self-assured and seemed to be someone who, one day, would be very important to the Doctor. She kept a diary of her experiences with the Doctor in his future, partly as a means of establishing where they were in his timeline each time they met. She also had a 'squareness gun' – the sonic blaster Captain Jack had left in the TARDIS – and an upgraded sonic screwdriver which the Doctor had given her the last time she'd seen him. Distrusted by the Doctor, River Song's proof that he would one day trust her absolutely was that she knew his real name – something he had never told anyone. Indeed, the Doctor said that he could think of only one occasion when he might tell anyone his name, though he did not specify when that might be. But it was enough to convince him she was telling the truth.

River Song demonstrated her loyalty to him when she prevented him risking his life to save everyone else. She knocked him out and wired herself into The Library's computer in his place. She was killed, but the Doctor realised that his future self had prepared for this – her sonic screwdriver contained a hidden neural relay that saved a copy of her living consciousness which he managed to transfer to The Library's Data Core, where she lived on in a virtual reality.

Story **The Doctor's Daughter** ❀ Written by **Stephen Greenhorn** ❀ Featuring **the Tenth Doctor, Donna and Martha** ❀ Foe **the Hath, General Cobb** ❀ First broadcast **10 May 2008** ❀ **1 episode**

Story **The Unicorn and the Wasp** ❀ Written by **Gareth Roberts** ❀ Featuring **the Tenth Doctor and Donna** ❀ Foe **the Vespiform** ❀ First broadcast **17 May 2008** ❀ **1 episode**

Story **Silence in the Library** and **Forest of the Dead** ❀ Written by **Steven Moffat** ❀ Featuring the Tenth Doctor and Donna ❀ Foe the Vashta Nerada ❀ First broadcast 31 May, 7 June 2008 ❀ **2 episodes**

What will you be?

After the liberation of the Ood-Sphere, Ood Sigma promised that his people would forever sing songs of 'the DoctorDonna', seemingly foreseeing what would happen when the Daleks constructed their Reality Bomb. Ood Sigma was not alone in intimating some terrible future for Donna – a Fortune Teller on Shan Shen fled in terror asking 'What are you? What will

you be?', and a servant at the Shadow Proclamation was sorry for 'the loss that is yet to come'. And, with the walls between realities crumbling, Rose Tyler returned to our universe and explained that a Dimension Cannon had revealed the time lines were all converging on Donna. Donna was about to become part of a complex and unique space-time event. When the Doctor's excess regeneration energy caused a two-way biological metacrisis between his spare hand and Donna, a new, part-human Doctor was brought into being. But the process also fed back into Donna, remaining inert until an electrical discharge sparked the Time Lord part of her mind into life. She gained all the Doctor's knowledge and, combining it with her own human imagination, she was able to overcome the Daleks. This knowledge was too much for her human brain, however, and would prove fatal. The only means of saving her was for the Doctor to remove from her mind all her memories of him and everything they had experienced together.

Donna had begun to change as soon as she met the Doctor, losing interest in trivia and gossip as she began to understand the extent of the universe – she had become a better person. Now, she had no knowledge that any of that had ever even existed, and no recollection that she had been, for a moment, the most important woman in the universe. The Doctor last saw Donna gossiping on the phone with one of her friends and wondering how she could have added planets in the sky to the list of events she had missed, along with the Sycorax attack, the Cyberman invasion and Daleks flying over London. She no longer even recognised him, and he warned her family that remembering any of it would kill her.

Yet Donna had already shown that she would always have the potential to do great things when a time beetle altered reality around her so she had never met the Doctor. Without her influence, the Doctor had died facing the Racnoss and was not there to save Earth from future attacks. In this different reality, Donna sacrificed herself to save the Doctor and so the world.

Story **Midnight** ☺ Written by **Russell T Davies** ☺ Featuring **the Tenth Doctor and Donna** ☺ Foe **Midnight monster** ☺ First broadcast **14 June 2008** ☺ 1 episode

Story **Turn Left** ☺ Written by **Russell T Davies** ☺ Featuring **the Tenth Doctor, Donna and Rose with Wilf, Sylvia and UNIT** ☺ Foe **the Trickster's Brigade** ☺ First broadcast **21 June 2008** ☺ 1 episode

SYLVIA AND WILF

Sylvia played by **Jacqueline King** Guest appearance **The Runaway Bride (2006)** First regular appearance **Partners in Crime (2008)** Last appearance **Journey's End (2008)** Wilf played by **Bernard Cribbins** First appearance **Voyage of the Damned (2007)** Last appearance **Journey's End (2008)**

Both Jacqueline King and Bernard Cribbins were initially cast in one-off appearances, but Catherine Tate's return in Series Four meant that Donna's family would be needed again. The newspaper seller from Voyage of the Damned became Donna's grandad after Howard Attfield, who had played Geoff Noble, became ill and was unable to return.

Sylvia first encountered the Doctor on Donna's aborted wedding day and was unimpressed by this madman warning of killer Christmas trees. She remained as wary of him as she was domineering to her daughter. But when the Doctor returned Donna home Sylvia showed how much she really cared for Donna, insisting her daughter was still the most important woman in the universe.

Sylvia's dad Wilf first met the Doctor exactly one year after Donna had, although none of them noticed this extra connection between the Doctor and Donna. Quietly amused by Sylvia and doting on Donna, Wilf was delighted and scared finally to be encountering the aliens that fascinated him.

Story **The Stolen Earth** and **Journey's End** ☻ Written by **Russell T Davies** ☻ Featuring **the Tenth Doctor, Donna, Martha, Captain Jack, Rose and Sarah Jane** with **Wilf, Sylvia, Francine, Jackie, Mickey, K-9 Mk IV** and **UNIT** ☻ Foe the **Daleks, Davros** ☻ First broadcast **28 June–5 July 2008** ☻ **2 episodes**

⬡ The Children of Time

The loss of Donna – predicted by Dalak Caan when he said that the Children of Time would gather and one of them would die – was one of several seemingly final farewells for the Doctor. The TARDIS had briefly been fully crewed for the first time in centuries but, with Earth returned to its natural orbit, each of the Doctor's friends left him once more: Sarah Jane Smith went back to her adopted son Luke in Ealing; Martha Jones, recently promoted to medical director by UNIT, left with Captain Jack Harkness, on his way back to Torchwood in Cardiff. Mickey Smith, no longer content to remain on the parallel Earth, went with them. Jackie Tyler, however, did go back to the other Earth, where Pete and her young son were waiting for her, and the Doctor insisted Rose would have to stay there too – there was now a duplicate Doctor who needed healing from the anger and hurt of war against the Daleks, but whose single human heart meant that he could properly share her life. His friends all gone, the Doctor resumed his travels alone…

TORCHWOOD

With Captain Jack Harkness in charge, the Cardiff branch of Torchwood had taken a very different path from the London version the Doctor encountered at Canary Wharf. Jack saw its role as preparing to protect the world from the dangers it would meet in the 21st century. By the time the Daleks invaded, he had recruited Gwen Cooper and Ianto Jones, who defended the Torchwood Hub from a Dalek attack when Jack used his transmat to join forces with the Doctor. They were able to use the Hub to boost Harriet Jones's Subwave Network signal to the Doctor, with help from Sarah Jane's supercomputer Mr Smith, and later fed power from Torchwood's Rift Manipulator to the TARDIS as it towed planet Earth back home.

JACKSON LAKE

Played by **David Morrissey** Guest appearance **The Next Doctor (2008)**

Knowing that David Tennant would be leaving the series after the completion of five special episodes, Russell T Davies decided that these last Tenth Doctor adventures would feature a series of guest stars rather than an ongoing companion. The first of these was David Morrissey, well known as a lead in Sense and Sensibility, State of Play and Blackpool (with David Tennant), whose role as – apparently – 'the next Doctor' was confirmed soon after the announcement of Tennant's departure.

Jackson Lake was a mathematics teacher from Sussex who was moving to London to take up a post at the University. He arrived in London in early December 1851 with his wife Caroline and their son Frederic and moved into 15 Latimer Street. There, in the cellars, he

discovered a squad of Cybermen which had fallen out of the Void and through time as the Daleks assembled their Reality Bomb. The Cybermen killed Caroline and abducted Frederic, leaving Lake behind.

But Jackson had found an Infostamp containing data about the Daleks which the Cybermen had stolen from the Daleks.

> Story **The Next Doctor** ✪ Written by **Russell T Davies** ✪ Featuring **the Tenth Doctor, Jackson and Rosita** ✪ Foe **the Cybermen** ✪ First broadcast **25 December 2008** ✪ 1 episode
>
> Story **Music of the Spheres** ✪ Written by **Russell T Davies** ✪ Featuring the Tenth Doctor and the Graske ✪ First broadcast 1 January 2009 ✪ 1 episode

The Infostamp backfired and streamed this data into Jackson's mind. He became convinced that he was the Doctor, charged with defending London against the Cybermen and their Cybershades before he could leave the city in his 'Tardis' – a hot-air balloon of his own invention. This Other Doctor armed himself with a screwdriver ('sonic' only because it made a noise) and set about hunting down the Cybermen. Aware that there were chunks of his memories missing, he put this down to the after-effects of regeneration, as did the real Doctor when he arrived and met what he at first took to be a future self.

Jackson Lake's innate intelligence and courage initially helped convince the Doctor that he had encountered a successor, and made the pair well matched as they faced Miss Hartigan and the Cyber King. Though Jackson was shattered by the revelation of what had truly happened to him and his family, he recovered quickly enough to realise that the true Doctor would now need his assistance. He was inventive, devising improvised solutions much as the Doctor did,

ROSITA FARISI

Saved from a Cyberman by a stranger calling himself the Doctor, Rosita found herself becoming the man's willing companion. Together they tried to track down and capture a Cybershade, Rosita entrusted with this Doctor's 'sonic screwdriver'. Fiercely loyal to this man who had saved her life, she was also quick to spot that there was something different about the next arrival – the real Doctor – appealing to him to help her own Doctor. She proved a resourceful ally to both men, rescuing them as a Cybershade dragged them through an empty warehouse and later repaying Miss Hartigan's insults with a punch in the mouth. She stayed with the Lakes as nursemaid for Frederic.

such as opening the core of an Infostamp, disabling its safety cutouts and using it as a weapon to immobilise Cybermen. And he was generous and compassionate, recognising the Doctor's loneliness and leading the London crowds in a rare moment of applause for the Doctor's efforts to save them. Unusually, he managed to persuade the Doctor to stay in London for long enough to enjoy Christmas dinner with him, Frederic and Rosita before resuming his travels.

LADY CHRISTINA DE SOUZA

Played by **Michelle Ryan** Guest appearance **Planet of the Dead (2009)**

The guest star for the first of 2009's special episodes was a high-profile actor who had found fame in a long-running role in EastEnders. Since leaving the soap opera, Michelle Ryan had taken the lead in a US revival of Bionic Woman, as well starring in BBC One's Jekyll, written by Steven Moffat, and in Merlin.

Christina was a bored aristocrat who'd taken to carrying out increasingly daring high-profile burglaries to get a bit of adventure into her life. Her latest haul was a priceless medieval drinking cup, stolen from London's International Gallery. She was witty, self-assured and inventive, devising extravagant and elaborate means of liberating priceless artefacts from behind layers of security. She had attracted the dogged attentions of a Detective Inspector McMillan, who was finally closing in on her. Then she met a madman on a London bus, just moments before the whole vehicle was transported through space to the desert world of San Helios. With no way back to Earth and under threat from alien predators, all they could rely on was the Doctor's experience, Christina's extensive collection of tools and their wits. Thankfully, she and the Doctor made the perfect team…

Story **Planet of the Dead** 😊
Written by **Russell T Davies &
Gareth Roberts** 😊 Featuring
the Tenth Doctor, Christina
and UNIT 😊 First broadcast
April 2009 😊 1 episode

UNIT

Confronted by the sight of an ordinary London bus disappearing through a freak wormhole, the police were out of their depth. UNIT quickly took control of the situation under the command of Captain Erisa Magambo. Though she had no knowledge of it, this was not Captain Magambo's first experience of events involving the Doctor – in the alternative reality built around Donna by the time beetle, Captain Magambo had worked with Rose Tyler to scavenge the dying TARDIS for the technology that took Donna back in time to reverse her fateful decision. Now, with no sign of the Doctor, Captain Magambo had to ready her forces against any alien attack from the wormhole, assisted by UNIT's current scientific adviser, Malcolm Taylor.